Desperate to Fly

Love and Soaring

are the Champagne of life

And thus intoxicated

Your soul can reach

Infinite heights

Desperate to Fly

By

Kai Gertsen

BT Link Publishing

Photographs reprinted courtesy Helga Gertsen,
John Seymour and Deborah Hudson.
Essays *Diamond in the East*, and *Appalachian Mission*,
reprinted courtesy Rochester Soaring Association.

Edited by Karin Schlösser

Cover design by Just Ink.
Cover photograph by Deborah Hudson

ISBN 978-0-9831306-1-1

Biography, Aviation, Adventure, History.

Printed in the United States of America

www.BTLinkpublishing.com

Contents

Foreword

We first met this Danish fellow at the airfield in Batavia, NY, sometime in 1956. Enthusiasm one might say—boundless enthusiasm for most things, especially for gliding machines and the people who flew them. It was the start of a friendship that lasted for decades and grew stronger with time.

In those days with little disposable income and glider performance to match, we had great fun in spite of it, and looking back, we had incredible dreams of sleek flying machines and flights to match. Helped of course by Kai's remarkable clairvoyance or perhaps his brand of "mind over matter" thinking. Often, while driving to the airport under grey skies and with intermittent windshield wipers, the Gertsen forecast was always "it's going to be good". And somehow, it usually was.

These memoirs are of the early years in Denmark, the Yukon, Canada, and finally in Rochester, NY. The chapters are remarkable in content, and with his flair for writing they come alive with detailed descriptions of life, and accounts of sometimes amazing adversity and triumph over the impossible. It is indeed a pity that Kai was unable to finish the chapter of the later years, and, as he said to me, "the really good stuff", referring to the contest flying in those sleek flying machines that we once only dreamed about, and to his love of family and friends. It is without saying however, that his many lifelong friends can help fill in the chapters not written with their own memories and stories about Kai and Helga, team Kilo India that could, and did it all.

—John Seymour SM

"Kilo India, Four Miles"

On the good days, the difficult days and the "totally hopeless" days, Kai always made it back from his soaring journeys. I often told him that when I found myself low with few to no options, I would ask myself "What would Kai do in this situation?" He always laughed his engaging laugh dismissing my assertion, but it was true. Kai had more focus and drive than anyone I know. His story told in this book demonstrates that.

Kai was a great friend and soaring companion as we explored the limitless skies together. He often commented how lucky we were to live just at this point in time when we have the technology, means and freedom to soar with the birds. We all miss his infectious presence and enthusiasm, but I miss it most of all when I soar away from Harris Hill on another journey through the sky.

—Tim Welles W3

Chapter 1

EARLY CHILDHOOD

I have no memories of my maternal grandfather, which is understandable as he died before I was born. From stories told about him during my childhood, it appears he was a "happy go lucky" fellow. He owned a small machine shop, but his genial personality proved to be somewhat detrimental to the balance sheet – he spent too much time "socializing" with his employees.

My paternal grandfather however is well entrenched in my memory. I have many fond memories from my early years of the many hours spent in my grandparents' apartment in Copenhagen, yet I know very little of my grand-father's life and experiences prior to that time.

Regarding my great-grandparents, I know nothing. I have pictures, but I have no idea what their life was like. What was their profession, their life experiences, hobbies and so on?

So that got me thinking about *my* grandkids. Perhaps I should leave them more than just a few pictures.

I have not accomplished any great deeds, but I have been fortunate to experience a wider spectrum of life than most of my contemporaries. Growing up in Copenhagen, I was exposed to the best of theater and sampled fine restaurants, I acquired hands-on experiences on a Danish farm, lived the life of early pioneers in the Yukon Territory, where I took on any job available while living in a shack without running water, got married to the best woman there ever was, and worked my way up from a penniless 19 year old to a respectable level in society, ultimately becoming part owner in a corporation. All this and having the good fortune of a lifetime of soaring – "The King of sports." It is not easy to envision a better life.

So here is my claim to fame: I have milked a cow, delivered water to Indians, and most importantly, I had an uncle who once rode on a street car with Victor Borge.

COPENHAGEN

I had the incredible good luck of being born and raised in a little town in Denmark called Copenhagen.

My parents owned and operated a delicatessen in Copenhagen. As the business was a full time job for both parents, I was raised by a nanny. My playground was the sidewalk and the back yard. The yard was no garden as the word implies in America, but a relatively small concrete area where trash cans and bicycles were kept, surrounded by tall buildings "Where the trash cans were kept" was not as bad as it sounds. First off, they were kept in an enclosed area. Moreover, it was customary to wrap one's garbage in newspaper, neatly tied up with a string which prevented the trash cans from getting soiled and did much to minimize the odor. Another interesting difference in custom from other countries was that on collection day trash cans were never placed on the street but retrieved by the trash collector from the rear of the buildings – it just didn't look right to have garbage cans in the street.

To my luck, there was a section of wall devoid of windows which was perfect for games of single handed catch. And when I got hungry, I would go to the store and mom would make me an open faced, lard-sandwich which consisted of a slice of hard dark bread with a generous application of pork lard and a liberal sprinkling of salt – a real treat.

I was as happy as the day was long.

MY PATERNAL GRANDPARENTS

I spent a great deal of time with my paternal grandparents. My grandfather was a bricklayer.

My grandparents lived in a third floor apartment in a working class neighborhood in the center of Copenhagen. It was a large apartment building, certainly over a hundred years old.

Many years later, on our visit there in 1972, it still looked just as I remembered; the bakery down the street where I went for fresh rolls and pastries on Sunday mornings, and the neat little park just around the corner still had the same old sand box that I played in all those years ago, and all completely unchanged. Everything neat and clean, and just like back then the sidewalks in front of the stores was washed every morning. It was as if time had stood still.

The apartment was quite nice, although the toilet was shared with the occupants in the next door apartment, and there was no bath tub or shower. The weekly trip to the local public bath took care of that.

Across from the entrance was the kitchen. All the other rooms were connected to a long hallway leading off to the right. The first room on the right was a generous sized parlor which was reserved for special celebrations like birthdays and holidays.

The parlor was where the piano lived. Culturally, it was almost mandatory back then for your children to learn to play the piano. My dad was tone deaf, but that was no reason not to have piano lessons. Despite this impediment, he did get to the point where he could pick out a tune. My mother was more talented. I remember she did quite a nice rendition of Liebestraum. After my grandparents passed on she never had access to a piano again which was really unfortunate.

The next door on the right was the dining room. It was a combination dining and family room, or as we called it "the every-day room". In addition to a dining table it was furnished with a couch and a writing desk. My grandfather was a foreman and apparently part of his job involved some kind of paper work as he spent quite a bit of time at his desk. The master bedroom was opposite the dining room and next to that, a second bedroom. The second bedroom was furnished with my great grandfather's bed, and was mine during my visits.

A single slim, elongated coal burning stove, located in a corner of the dining room, provided heat for the entire apartment. Each apartment had their assigned coal bin in the basement which was accessible by a narrow, spiral staircase at the back of the kitchen. Whenever I was there in wintertime it was my job to fetch the coal. Neither the basement nor the spiral staircase leading down to it had much light, so the lively imagination of a child made this task very exciting.

THE PARTIES

Danish people love parties and never miss an opportunity to have one. No birthday will go by uncelebrated.

My grandparents sure had some grand parties. Generally about a dozen guests were accommodated. Now that I think about it, no cocktails were ever served before dinner, but that didn't mean there were no worthwhile liquid refreshments with the meal. At these parties my grandparents engaged a distant aunt to do all the cooking and serving, allowing them to enjoy themselves. Dinner always consisted of four or five courses, supplemented with beer and Aquavit. The table was set with the finest china, either Bing & Grøndal or Royal Copenhagen. There must have been some working people households that didn't possess a complete set of one or the other, but I never got to know of any. Of course, the beverages were served in the finest crystal. The ladies were all in their evening gowns and the men in their finest. Everyone smoked. I didn't notice it then, but the smoke in that apartment must have been thick enough to choke an alligator, as there was no ventilation. Dinner was a three hour plus affair with a smoking recess between each course. After dinner everyone retired to the parlor for coffee, served with a selection of fine liqueurs.

This all seemed normal to me. Only much later in life did I discover that there are countries in the world where the working class does not live quite as well. Incredibly, all this entertaining took place during the great depression. Apparently, the Danes that decided to emigrate left their country not so much to find a more comfortable lifestyle, instead they must have been in search of excitement and adventure.

When my grandparents had their parties, they did it with elegance, but they were not frivolous with their money. Consequently, they had enough savings to set up my parents in a business when they got married.

The apartment had been my grandparent's home since they got married. I do not believe they ever added a new piece of furniture in all the years they lived there. Yet, none of it looked shabby.

STAYING WITH MY GRANDPARENTS

From time to time I would visit my grandparents and spend several days with them. Despite their frugality, they bought one toy for me to play during my visits; a wooden train set. I also had a set of tin soldiers and Indians (now that I think about it, they might have been clay) to entertain myself with. Those had belonged to my dad and uncle when they were kids, and it is a fair guess that these were *their* only purchased toys. Then there were many happy hours making paper airplanes and kites, and many futile attempts at launching the kites on the sidewalk. Another special treat on those mini vacations was orange soda. Such things were not daily fair at home.

There were two events I always looked forward to. One was laundry day. Every household was assigned one day a month to have use of the laundry room which was located in the loft. That was some loft. It was enormous, a great place for a young boy to explore. Certain areas were set aside to hang up the clothes for drying.

Now that I think about it, there were no outdoor clothes lines in Denmark; I never saw any clothes hung out to dry in the open anywhere. Even on more recent travel to Denmark we noticed that state of affairs still holds true. When people dry their laundry, the clothes lines are well hidden from public view.

The other special treat was when my grandfather took me along to his work site. With all the lumber, nails, and tools I had no trouble entertaining myself; the days were never long enough. I actually got quite good at ax throwing.

Once in a while, on the way home, we would visit a pub to meet some of his friends. My grandfather would have a few beers, play a little billiard, and I would have one of my favorite orange sodas. Grandma didn't think much of those excursions.

At the work site they had a shed where the men had lunch and kept their work clothes. Lunch usually consisted of open faced sandwiches brought from home in a specially designed lunch box that had shelves to prevent the sandwiches from getting squashed. Maintaining a change of clothes at work was necessary. None of the workers would ever consider being seen in their work clothes on a public street or street car on the way to and from work.

CHRISTMAS

Christmas was pure magic. It was always celebrated at my grandparent's home, and I would stay at their apartment a few days in advance of the holiday.

My grandmother would take me on a tour of the big department stores. Decorations and displays were put up a couple of weeks before Christmas, and they were fantastic. I distinctly remember one exceptional display in one of the major department stores which I had great difficulty tearing myself away from; a huge model harbor well stocked with all kinds of ships navigating the water through lift bridges.

The Christmas tree was purchased at a corner vendor a few days before Christmas Eve. We made the tree decorations ourselves, which consisted of paper cones cut out of sheets of craft paper, then glued in a cone shape. In accordance with Danish tradition, a few raisins and nuts were placed at the bottom of each cone for a special treat on Christmas Eve.

In Denmark Christmas is celebrated on the evening of the 24th. There are two traditional Christmas dinners; pork roast or goose. We always had pork roast. During the war, we used to lament as to how this might well be our last pork roast Christmas dinner, but every year we somehow managed to secure one more. Part of the traditional dinner was rice pudding for dessert. This was made of the left over rice from the dinner the day before, reinforced with a healthy portion of whipped cream; we simply could not conceive of Christmas without this delicacy. One single whole almond was added to the bowl, and the lucky one who got it was awarded the "Almond Prize" which was a confectionary marzipan pig. Then the candles were lit on the tree, and we sang Christmas songs and carols. Then finally, it was time to open the presents.

The next day, Christmas day, there was an elaborate lunch consisting of what in Denmark is known as a "cold table with warm dishes (fares)", perhaps better translated as "cold and warm fares". This typically consisted of pickled herring and other canned or smoked fish, a choice of salads, small warm beef fillets, various cold cuts, different type of breads, and different kinds of cheeses. All of this accompanied by beer and Aquavit. The Aquavit is served in a liqueur style glass. In accordance with tradition it is consumed in one swallow, and cannot be sipped. Being thrifty, my grandfather's Schnapps glasses were the smallest glasses available, probably less than half an ounce. His reasoning was this; a Schnapps is a Schnapps, the smaller the glass, the more drinks you get out of a bottle. I still have one of those glasses, and apply the same logic.

Christmas was pure magic.

THE END OF AN ERA

One night we got a call from the hospital. My grandfather had been critically injured during an explosion at work. It was a terrible blow. We frantically dressed and were on our way to the hospital in record time.

As it turned out, my grandfather had been erecting a wall in the factory and he was the only one left at work when it happened. Apparently the factory was engaged in some kind of business with the Germans. When saboteurs arrived to blow up the building, they called out to be sure no one was left on the premises, but my grandfather didn't hear them. He suffered severe burns over 90% of his body. His last words to me were that he was so happy I had not become a brick layer. Thankfully he died a few hours later.

MY MATERNAL GRANDPARENTS

As I mentioned, my maternal grandfather died fairly young. My grandmother remarried and I do not have a lot of memories of her second husband. He was a caretaker at a consulate, where they had a beautiful large apartment on the lower level. The estate had a great garden and whenever I was there, which wasn't too often, that is where I spent most of my time. I never was very close to my new paternal grandfather. He suffered terribly from sugar diabetes, and passed away in 1939.

SCHOOL DAYS

For my first three grades I went to school in Copenhagen. I went to the school by street car, which involved one transfer. I don't recall that ever creating any problems.

Cleanliness and proper manners, although not a subject in itself, were part of the curriculum. Of course in today's world this would be an intolerable invasion of individual rights. First thing in the morning we all lined up for inspection of clean finger nails. For those who did not meet the standard, there was a sink in the corner with a nail brush. Hats were not permitted; this was not a problem, as entering a building wearing a hat was totally inconceivable to any of us. Chewing gum in class was a fantasy you could not even fathom, and slouching was not tolerated. Prior to school trips we were lectured on the unacceptable act of littering.

As might be expected, all this indoctrination had a terrible everlasting impact on me as these "bad" habits stayed with me the rest of my life. To this day I cannot force myself to throw the tiniest piece of paper on the ground, anywhere, and it has been a lifelong habit to keep my fingernails clean at all times ever since.

In spite of this regiment, my school days were extraordinarily happy. There was one minor setback; I had red hair which made me a target to be picked on now and then, but I always recovered quickly. It simply wasn't in my nature to be upset for long.

It was either second or third grade when I had my moment in the spot light. It was in arithmetic class. For some reason the teacher called me to the blackboard and asked me for the answer of seven times seven, even though we had not yet gotten to that time table. Well, I just stood there quietly and added seven, seven times and came up with the correct answer. The teacher pulled out his purse and handed me a nickel and I was the proudest kid in school that day. I have no idea why he did this. Maybe he had noticed my lack of interest in studying and tried to light a fire. Too bad he didn't succeed.

COUNTRY LIFE

The idea was that time in the country would be a good experience for a city boy, and it so happened that a great aunt on my dad's side was married to a farmer in Jutland, the Danish mainland. The other attraction for me, being an only child, was that Rasmus and Martine had five children, two boys and three girls.

So at the prime age of six, my parents put me on a train in Copenhagen, with my small suitcase in hand and a sign around my neck listing my destination. I had to change trains a few times and the trip included a ferry ride as well. This was not really as big a deal for me as one might suspect. What helped considerably was that from the first day in school I rode the street car and the trip involved one transfer. The trip to my vacation fairyland was really not that much different other than that there were a few more segments and they were a little longer. You would think I would have had some apprehension about undertaking such a trip, but I do not recall any. For me it was incredibly exciting. The enormous size of the train station, the huge massive steam powered locomotives sitting there hissing, huffing and puffing, oozing clouds of steam – roaring to go. The adventure and excitement of it was delectable.

On my first trip I couldn't read and was obliged to depend on helpful strangers to come to my aid when changing trains and getting onto the ferry. Subsequently, I made that trip by myself every summer throughout the war years till I was 14 years old. It was a different story with my mother. She actually got sick with worry. What made it even more troublesome was that long distance phone calls were not made frivolously. I suppose if I had ever failed to arrive she would have received a telegram. The news of a successful, uneventful trip however would reach her by letter a week or so later.

So began my love affair with country life and farming. For the next eight

17

years I longed for these summer vacations. That was the life. My alarm clock on the farm consisted of horseshoe clatter on cobble stones as the horses were being prepared for the day's work and led to the water trough which was located in the middle of the farm yard. What a delightful wake-up call for another day in paradise.

Rasmus and Martine owned a typical Danish farm. It consisted of four large buildings forming a square with a large courtyard in the center. All the buildings were constructed of brick and had steep gables, ideal for hay storage, and were covered with thatched roofs. To my dismay, a few years after my first visit the thatched roofs were replaced by tin which I thought greatly diminished the appeal of the buildings. I must have sensed the end to an era. With all the hay stored in the lofts above the three work buildings, there was no need for a barn. I have never seen a barn in Denmark.

The building facing the road had a large arched entryway which led into the center courtyard. The rooms on either side of the entryway were used to store farm equipment. Leaving farm equipment out-doors exposed to the elements was unthinkable.

As you entered the courtyard, the building on the right housed the stalls for the horses and other livestock. Stalls for the dairy cows and the pig pens were located in the building on the left. These three building were connected.

The fourth building, a free standing building facing you as you entered the courtyard, was living quarters, known as "stuehuset". The house had two entrances facing the court yard. The one on the right led to three good sized bedrooms which were connected to the other end of the house by a long corridor. The separate external door was convenient as the outhouse was located on that side. The main entrance on the left led to the dining room and the kitchen.

The dining room was the every-day room where lunches and dinners were served. This was also where the piano was located. The oldest daughter, Dorte was the piano player. Sometimes in the evening she would play some of the old Danish folk songs and those of us who felt so inclined would sing along.

The kitchen was enormous, covering the full width of the house. In the back corner was a small bedroom which was occupied by the two sons. I think I was about 11 years old when I was moved from the luxurious bedrooms where the girls resided and in with the boys where hay served as a mattress; apparently boys were not to be pampered. Then there was the room reserved for special occasions, which was large enough to comfortably accommodate twenty or so people. It was an elegantly furnished living room with a good sized dining table. Regrettably, I did not get a picture of that living room when we made a return visit in 1972, but I did take a picture of the parlor at the farm of their eldest daughter who by that time had settled in a nearby village, just to give you a feel for how it looked back then.

Behind 'stuehuset' was the garden which was meticulously kept and lovingly cared for. In the center of the garden stood a flag pole, not a rusty piece of pipe, but the real thing. Of course, the flag was only flown on special occasions such as birthdays or national holidays, and always lowered at sunset and properly folded.

The neatness and cleanliness of the farm was not exceptional, it was pretty much standard all throughout the Danish countryside.

You may think these are all embellished childhood memories, but I checked the accuracy of my recollection when we visited in 1972 and everything was pretty much still as I have described.

FARM LIVING

We ate well. Breakfast was served after milking time, at about 6 am, and well worth waiting for. The prime sustaining dish consisted of a thick slice of hard rye bread, cut into small cubes, served in a bowl with warm milk. This was followed by fresh homemade bread with various kinds of jams and cheeses.

Incidentally, the cooking was done on a wood burning stove, with peat blocks being used as fuel. This was another task I got acquainted with; cutting blocks of peat out of the bog and stacking them in small, pyramid shaped piles to dry.

My favored lunch was fried bacon, sliced about 3/8 of an inch thick with small potatoes and white gravy. On our visit in 1972 they were very eager to please us and asked what I would like for dinner. There was no hesitation; bacon with new potatoes and white gravy. Martine objected, "but that is just an every-day meal, we want to prepare something special," I tried to convince her that this *was* special. She shook her head, but obliged, and I was not disappointed.

During the war years there was another major attraction to being on a farm; there was plenty of food. That is not to say that we were starving in the city, but there were times when we had to resort to go out in the potato fields and scrounge for leftovers after harvest.

During these summer vacations, I didn't *have* to do anything, but it was great fun to participate in all the chores and I didn't miss out on any. I learned to milk cows, sitting on a milking stool with a bucket between my legs, leaning the top of my head against the cow's belly. I even had the honor to help pluck a chicken. Of course, the fact that I didn't *have* to do anything made it so much more appealing.

I consider myself very fortunate to have experienced that era. Now a great deal of the romance of farming has been lost. A short time after the war, horses were replaced by tractors. By the eighties, every dairy operation in Denmark with 25 or more cows was totally automated and computer controlled.

One incident sticks in my mind as if it happened yesterday. I had cleaned out the cow stalls and Rasmus was so impressed with the job, that with a display of pomp he pulled out his purse and gave me a dime. I went down to the town store (there was only one) and purchased a chocolate frog - dark chocolate in the shape of a frog with peppermint filling - the best treat I have ever had.

A lot of time was spent in the potato and turnip fields, turning the dirt around the plants with a hoe. The highlight of working in the fields occurred mid-morning when the women showed up with coffee and freshly baked pastry and we settled down in the hedge row to enjoy these treats. Baking good pastry was taken seriously and the result was accordingly; mouthwatering. Not to be confused with Danish pastry U.S. style.

Incidentally, coffee was seldom served without pastry. In 1972 when we were on a picnic with Helga's cousin, husband, and kids we stopped for a cup of coffee by the side of the road. When it became obvious that we were only having coffee, the kids exclaimed "What! Cake-less coffee?"

The biggest thrill was harvest time. I recall riding on top of the hay wagon, holding on as it rocked from side to side, being drawn by horses. I can still remember the sweet scent of fresh mowed hay. What indescribable, pure pleasure.

Lunch was always followed by a half hour nap. The evenings were sacred, strictly reserved for relaxation. And they complained about their life and how they had to slave, always going on about the soft and easy life of city folk (I was pondering that many years later when I worked in a Ford plant in Buffalo, NY, ten hours a day with a 20 minute break for lunch, and one day off every two weeks.)

A day seldom went by when we did not go for a swim in the creek which meandered through the fields just 400 yards behind the farm. The generous measure of mud was no deterrent. The creek was also a treasure trove when it came to fishing for eels. This was a fairly simple operation whereby one would walk through the reeds stirring up the eels with bare feet, scaring them into a rectangular net. In about 20 minutes we could gather enough eels for a mouth-watering dinner.

When I was not busy with chores, I had two favored places to occupy my time. There was a duck pond out back that I took great pleasure in draining, cleaning and refilling. And when I wasn't busy at the pond, they could find me perched high in one of the trees that surrounded the garden, contemplating life and enjoying the beauty of it all.

However, there was one event I wish I would have missed, and that was the slaughter of a pig. Regrettably, that picture is also flawlessly imprinted in my mind and it is a mystery why I am not a confirmed vegetarian. I must be the ultimate hypocrite. I must say, not much of that pig was wasted. Most of the meat was salted, the head was used for head cheese, tongue, liver, kidneys and the hoofs were considered delicacies, and the blood was made into blood sausages, which I never did grow fond of.

Another experience I would just as soon forget about was a toothache. To fully comprehend the cure for a toothache it is necessary to describe the smoking habits on the farms at that time. Tobacco was enjoyed by using a pipe with a bowl, the size of a small space heater, resting on the floor, with a long stem enabling the user to smoke from a comfortable position in his easy chair. Occasionally the bowl was cleaned and the residual was deposited in a special drawer where it was mixed with a bit of tobacco. Whenever Rasmus felt like a special treat he would take a pinch or two and embed it in his cheeks. So the treatment for my tooth ache was a wad of that concoction being placed on the tooth and then soaked with a shot of Aquavit – I forgot all about my tooth ache.

During the war when tobacco was in short supply, it was incredible what some people would do to get a smoke. Once we visited a distant relative, also a farmer, who had resorted to smoking rhubarb leaves; he had rows of them strung out in his loft for drying. When he stoked up his pipe everyone had to evacuate the house, as it smelled like old mattresses on fire.

In 1939, I was treated to a less complicated, more straightforward journey to my summer playground. In the evening my parents dropped me off at a steam ship in the Copenhagen harbor. No trains or ferry, but a direct over-night voyage. The following morning Rasmus and Martine met me at the dock in Aalborg with their spotless 1937 Chevrolet, complete with a small vase of fresh flowers on the dash for the special occasion. Needless to say, they were dressed in their finest.

How they dressed sticks in my mind. When a farmer went out on the town, the last thing he wanted to do was look like one. In a restaurant or a movie theater you could not tell a farmer from a lawyer.

Just because of my euphoric accounts of the happy vacations at the farm, don't get the wrong impression that I was unhappy the rest of the time. I had an extremely happy childhood. This was due both to my cheerful disposition as well as my parents' indifference to education. I managed to convince them that schools no longer required students to do homework, and they never pressed the issue. Consequently I had a great time; nothing but play. Not surprisingly, my grades suffered accordingly.

THE WAR

Then came one of the darkest days in Denmark's history; April 9, 1940. The first we knew something was wrong was about eight in the morning when the sky grew dark. We looked out the window and there were airplanes, wing to wing from horizon to horizon – the Germans had arrived. As much as we didn't like it, there was not much we could do. Our armed forces were pathetic. I believe the Danish Air Force consisted of two airplanes and one was destroyed on the ground that day. The other took off, but was called back as there was simply no point to risking it in action. At first, there was fighting near the Danish-German border, but the German forces were formidable. The Germans presented an ultimatum, which if not accepted would mean massive aerial attacks, and after a 5 hours confrontation the fighting ended. Thus we avoided the total destruction of our cities, which became the fate of many other European countries.

As happens all too often, we were too hasty in our judgment. At first, we believed that the Germans had their heart in the right place and came with perfectly good intentions. Hitler himself stated that he only moved his troops into Denmark to protect and safeguard us from the Allies. Thus the German forces called themselves "Wærnemagten" (The Protective Power). But there was a problem; we had not asked for their protection.

As the war progressed, rationing and restrictions grew more severe and everything became scarce. Ordering an open faced sandwich in a restaurant required a wad of rationing cards, specific cards for each ingredient; one for the bread, one for butter, pork, chicken, cheese and so forth. There was not a single item that did not require a rationing card and they were as valuable as money.

In 1943 the Nazis attempted to break the Danes spirit by burning down the concert hall in their beloved Tivoli Garden. They didn't succeed, as a temporary building was erected within weeks and the park was back in operation.

On October 2, 1943 an order was issued to arrest all Jews. Fortunately, a civil servant within the German administration leaked the plan to the Danish resistance, and they succeeded in passing on a warning to about 7,000 Jews. Some of the Jews warned could not believe the Germans would commit such an act and refused to flee or go into hiding. As a result, 475 Danish Jews were captured and shipped to concentration camps in Germany. The few that returned after the war had their prisoner number branded on their upper arm. Some of the Jewish nationals that received advance notice of the German raid went into hiding, assisted by their non-Jewish friends, but eventually most escaped to Sweden via fishing boats arranged for by the Danish resistance movement. Judging by how few were apprehended while crossing the sea to Sweden, it is tempting to believe that some of the German patrols looked the other way.

The war must have been a traumatic experience for my parents, but for a teenage boy it was more exciting than scary. Many night hours were spent in the bomb shelter which in our case was the basement.

Because my Dad had a problem serving the German occupying forces, my parents had to give up the deli. He found a job as superintendent of a new apartment complex in a little town just north of Copenhagen by the name of Lyngby.

Kai Gertsen

TIVOLI

In 1843, while the rest of Europe was embroiled in wars and revolutions, the Danes busied themselves with the building of an amusement park; Tivoli Gardens, located in the center of Copenhagen.

This world renowned park exudes a cheerful, charming and romantic ambience. Although it dates back over one and a half centuries, a few of the original attractions remain unchanged to this day. It has, of course, kept in step with the changing times, but still the special allure remains.

Aside from the usual amusement rides, this unique theme park offers all kinds of entertainment such as circus performances, top rated restaurants, and a classical concert hall featuring performances by leading European orchestras and the best solo musicians.

From when I was very little till about five or six years old, our first stop when visiting Tivoli was the Pantomime Theatre where I would sit in one of the first rows. This theatre was built in 1874 and remains unchanged to this day. It has been home to the Italian Pantomime "Commedia dell'Arte," and the characters of their plays are the same today as on opening night well over a hundred years ago.

BAKKEN

There were also many trips to Dyrehavsbakken, or "Bakken" (The Hill), as it was mostly referred to, another amusement park located 8 miles north of Copenhagen. It was founded in 1756, which makes it the oldest amusement park in the World. It was not as sophisticated as Tivoli, but did include 40 restaurants serving delicious Danish fare and is home to the Circus Revue, the biggest and funniest revue in Denmark.

When I was 12 years old, I decided on an alternate profession in case I could not become a pilot, which was my dream since I was born. My cousin and I envisioned spending all our time riding on roller coaster rides. At that time it was a law that every roller coaster train had to have a brake-man. The brake-man's spot was in the last car and he just sat there all day ready to apply the brake, which of course he never did or the cars wouldn't get back to start. Just imagine; riding a roller coaster all day and getting paid for it. That definitely had to be the best job in the world next to being a pilot.

One of the most popular features was *the* ice cream stand - there was only one. Nobody went to Bakken without getting an ice cream cone, and this was no ordinary ice cream either! The waffle cone was warm, right out of the waffle iron, filled with ice cream topped with berries and piled high with whipped cream. On a recent trip to Denmark I made the disheartening discovery that this

23

very special ice cream stand now only exists in my memory.

Naturally, our paths inevitably lead us by one of the beer halls where my dad and uncle had to stop for a draft of premium Danish beer. I have fond memories of the many happy hours at that special place.

As delightful as those places were, I am thankful that my exposure to Danish culture was not limited to Bakken and Tivoli. My parents treasured the night life of Copenhagen, and from the age of 10 they would take me along from time to time. Thus, I am very fortunate to have experienced the best of theater, operettas, music and the finest restaurants in this most prominent city in Europe.

SKIING & SKATING

Our skiing back then was a bit different from what they do today. First off, the equipment was rather primitive. I got my skis from my aunt who got them from a Finnish soldier; they were twice as long as I was tall. There was a rectangular hole in the ski for a strap to go through which then went over the toe of my boot. The boots were plain ordinary boots, not special ski boots. Lateral control was nonexistent; standing on the skis I could turn my feet 90 degrees one way and the other while the skis remained straight.

It wasn't often that we got enough snow for skiing, but when we did we would not let it go to waste. We would strap on our skis and head out for the one skiing hill in the area. This particular hill, really a farmer's field, would hardly excite any skier today, but we didn't know any better. On one side we herring-boned up, on the other we went down, and half way down was a ski-jump.

I had my heart set on ski-jumping, but my chances of success were remote. As I got airborne my skis would do their own thing. Not being restricted by firm bindings, they would invariably blow and drift every which-way after leaving the jump. I rarely landed on my feet, and most of the time everything turned white as I made contact with the ground. In accordance with Einstein's definition of being crazy - doing the same thing over and over with the same negative result -, I qualified.

Once in a while I would ski down the more mundane part of the hill. With my version of bindings I could only go straight, and stopping was accomplished by falling down. We looked in dismay at the people who made turns all the way down, figuring they made all those turns because they were afraid to go fast.

If there wasn't enough snow for skiing, the ice on the lake was usually thick enough to go skating. Like my skiing equipment, my skates were hardly up-to-date. The skates were attached to your shoes by two pair of prongs, fore and aft, which clamped onto the sole of your shoes. The prongs were operated by a key which invariably got lost from time to time. As might be expected, the sole eventually separated from the shoes, but we manage to glue them back together before our parents found out.

Sometimes one of us showed up without skates. No problem, we shared and two of us would be skating on one skate. We weren't too particular.

GAMES

Luckily, I was able to put all that extra play time gained by not doing homework to better use such as building and sailing model sailboats, playing soccer, (not the serious, organized kind, but just a bunch of kids kicking a ball around, using two rocks for goal posts), roaming in the woods, climbing trees, or playing Tarzan and making bows and arrows from Weeping Willow branches. Or playing Indians or making wooden swords to arm Robin Hood and his men. Daredevil deeds such as climbing on the underside of railroad bridges or running along the tracks knowing that a train may come at any time would boost our adrenalin whenever needed.

I only remember two toys, other than the ones at my grandparent's house. My favorite was a Meccano Erector Set. It was possible to build just about anything with these parts; cars, cranes, etc. I think there were a total of about ten different sets and if you had all ten you could build the Tower Bridge of London. So that was my life's dream at the time, to get all ten sets. Dreams are of a fleeting nature, they come and go and are seldom realized.

The other toy allowed us to play a game that entertained us endlessly, but it required two players. It was a small toy airplane, the type you hold in your hand and your imagination does the rest. One would hold the model and pretend to be flying on instruments. This was accomplished by the "pilot" closing his eyes. The other would be "ground control" and direct him to the "airfield", turn right, go straight, descend, level off, etc.

A stack of ordinary playing cards could entertain us for hours. We would get as many decks as we could find and build a card house in one corner of the room. Then we constructed a "fuse" which went all around the perimeter of the room. This "fuse" consisted of a series of two cards leaning against one another in the shape of a steeple; they were spaced close enough to cause a domino effect if one was to fall over. Needles to say the fuse was sensitive, and to prevent premature activation we would leave a gap at reasonable intervals. Still, it was a tense situation; it only took someone entering the room to trigger a catastrophe and we would have to start all over again or at least reconstruct a good portion of it. But, of course, that was part of the fun.

HALLOWEEN

Halloween was a delight. In Denmark, the holiday is celebrated in late February, and every year I was a pirate. The costume was made from bits and pieces, whatever was readily available. Eyebrows were darkened with soot from a burned cork. Trick 'n treat time was Saturday and Sunday from mid morning to mid afternoon. The treats consisted of coins. Each of us had a tin can with a slot in the lid, which we would rattle as we approached our "victims." The only exception was the bakeries. There we sang a traditional song, the lyrics warning of mischief if we didn't get some pastry, and we usually got some. Sunday we quit trick 'n treating a little earlier so we could get to the movie theater in time for the afternoon matinee, which was usually a Laurel and Hardy or similar fare. A worthwhile way to spend our loot.

SWIMMING

With lakes and the ocean nearby, a lot of time was spent swimming. None of us had the advantage of formal swim instruction, but that didn't seem to be a problem.

While in 7th grade as we walked to school on winter mornings, we would see a man on his bicycle with a towel in the front basket returning from his swim in the ocean – I was inspired. No reason I couldn't do that! I laid out my plan for the following year. It was quite simple; at the end of the summer I would establish a rigid schedule of going for a swim every single day. My reasoning was this, if you went swimming one day there was no reason why you couldn't go the next day – the trick was not to miss a day. The drop in temperature would be so gradual it would scarcely be noticeable – perfectly logical. So at the end of the summer I put my plan into action. Regardless of weather, I peddled out to the ocean for my daily dip. I managed to do this for quite some time, well into the fall. But then for some reason beyond my control I missed two days in a row. Just then the weather turned particularly nasty, and I lost interest – I suppose I will never join a polar bear club.

CULTURAL DIFFERENCES

I have to make one more observation regarding the difference in cultures. In Denmark, at least at that time, it was acceptable to consume beer in the work place, except for apprentices. The factory where I served my apprenticeship had a small shop that offered coffee, pastries, cookies and beer. Midmorning and mid afternoon the shop keeper would load up his little cart with a variety of goodies including beer, and make the rounds. There were few beer sales mid-morning, but sales were brisk in the afternoon. Inevitably, sales peaked at noon as no self-respecting Dane would consider eating lunch without a beer.

There once was an interesting episode at a building site where my bricklayer grandfather worked. The owner of the building project decided there was to be no more beer drinking on his building site. He took it upon himself to climb up the ladder and kick a case of beer off a scaffold – all work stopped immediately. This created a situation which was not negotiable for the men. He finally agreed to have the case of beer replaced, but that was not good enough. He had to carry the case of beer up the scaffold himself, nothing less would do. He had no choice – a bitter pill to swallow, no doubt.

In spite of the war, I had a very happy childhood. I don't recall ever being depressed about anything. When the war ended and I discovered how many people suffered unimaginable hardships, I almost developed a guilt complex for having had such a marvelous time; it just did not seem fair.

1929

My grandfather, 4th from left, with his bricklayer buddies

My Dad

Mom and I

In Copenhagen

My maternal grandparents
(Typical working class attire)

School in Copenhagen

Pantomime Theatre, Tivoli. Unchanged since the opening in 1847.

Italian Commedia Dell'arte

In Copenhagen with my paternal grandmother

On a picnic with my grandparents, dad by me

The farm, my second home

We did our best to look debonair

A typical parlor on a Danish farm

Rasmus and Martine, my vacation parents

Happy days on the farm 1936

The town of Vester Alling. 'Our' farm, upper left.

At about eight years old

A day at the beach. My aunt (my mother's sister) on the left

Chapter 2

DISCOVERING GLIDING

Exactly one month after I was born, a historic milestone in gliding history was reached.

On May 15, 1929 Robert Kronfeld flew his Wien sailplane on a 102.2km cross-country soaring flight, breaking the 100km barrier. Of course, this was of no interest to me at the time, but by the time I was fifteen I started to read everything I could get my hands on about the achievements and adventures of soaring pilots.

I always felt I was born too late. In my opinion, the 1930s were by far the most exciting period in gliding with improvements in design and pilot performance advancing at an extraordinary pace. As it turned out, I did have the good fortune to participate in the world of gliding from the mid 40's on, although about four years were lost due to circumstances beyond my control.

I was obsessed with flying from the moment I was born. This is curious as neither my parents, nor any of my other relatives for that matter, had any interest in aviation what so ever. Perhaps I am a reincarnated hawk who wanted to be a glider pilot the next time around.

At the age of four I could be seen running along the sidewalks of Copenhagen in a futile attempt to launch my pathetic paper kites. While other kids put chairs together to play train, I assembled crates, which were in abundant supply at my parent's delicatessen, in the shape of an airplane. Later, I spent endless hours by the seashore enthralled by the soaring flight of seagulls along the sand dunes.

Had I gazed skyward from my playground in Copenhagen on the 7th of June 1936, I might have caught a glimpse of Peter Riedel flying his Rhönsperber above the city on a flight that originated in Malmö, Sweden; the first real soaring flight over open water, crossing Øresund which is a body of water nine miles wide. The earlier two English Channel crossings by Kronfeld in 1931, one in each direction, were glides from high altitude tows. Believe it or not, these high tows were allowed by the rules for the £1,000 prize offered by the Daily Mail.

Had I seen the Rhönsperber back then, it would have saved me the trouble of trying to "invent" a glider using wooden crates when I was a young boy. Many years later, I had the privilege of meeting Peter Riedel during the 1959 U.S.

National Contest on Harris Hill, and we had a discussion on the technique of centering thermals.

MODEL GLIDERS

Early on during WW II, my parents sold the delicatessen and we moved to Lyngby, a little town 20 miles north of Copenhagen where my dad was hired to fill the position of superintendent of an apartment complex.

Summer vacations were spent on my uncle's farm, but when school was in session I often went hiking by myself on the weekends. One day in 1942, on one of my lone escapades, I was hiking through an open area (Eremitagesletten) in a park north of Copenhagen by the name of Dyrehaven when I came across two grown-up men playing with their model gliders, and I was hooked.

In our apartment building every apartment was assigned a storage cubicle in the basement. Ours had been converted into a work shop. The day after that hike, the workshop production shifted from model sailboats to model gliders.

The first model was constructed from plans which I obtained through a magazine. It was huge, to me at least. Surely bigger would be better. It took three months of all my free time to build, I was proud of it and thought it really looked impressive. Before I put the covering on, that is. Once the covering was on, it was another story. I didn't know that the model had to be pinned down and rigidly restrained during the shrinking process of the covering to prevent warping. Now my super model more closely resembled a pretzel. In a fit of temper I destroyed the whole thing – the one and only time I ever lost my temper. Nonetheless, within a week I was back in full swing building another, but of more modest proportions.

CONFIRMATION

At the age of 14 it was time for confirmation.

Our abode was a rather small one bedroom apartment, but where there is a will there is a way. The bedroom furniture was moved to the basement. A 'U' shaped table was constructed from saw horses and plywood, and once decorated with our finest silverware, crystal wineglasses, and Royal Copenhagen dishes, it was a table fit for royalty.

Confirmation was the time when a boy transitioned into manhood. In accordance with the traditional rituals required to make this transformation, my proud father offered me a beer, a shot of Aquavit, and a cigarette. I had no problem with the beer and Aquavit, but I did have a problem with the cigarette; I had to pretend I hadn't smoked before. Apparently I handled the situation well enough – I was now a man.

Once the 3 hour dinner was over the carpet in the living room was rolled up to make room for dancing. In Denmark (at that time) a party was not a party without dancing. It was a marvelous affair.

CAREER PLANNING

When I was 12 years old my dad made arrangements for a toolmaker apprenticeship to start when I turned 16, which was the youngest age an apprenticeship could commence. "If you have a trade, you can always make a decent living" was my dad's reasoning. "If you want to do something else you can do that later, but you will always have a trade to fall back on" – the die was cast.

There was something to be said for this arrangement; I didn't have to go out and find myself, ponder who I was or what I was going to do. The problem was that I already knew exactly what I wanted to do with my life. My only interest was flying and I desperately wanted to become an airline pilot. I had no interest whatsoever in becoming a toolmaker, but I had no say in the matter.

Becoming a pilot remained an obsession, but did I have the abilities? I was eager to find out. At that time the Polytechnic Institute of Copenhagen offered a vocational aptitude test and I signed up. It was an all-day affair and the result was positive. Yes, I had all the physical and mental qualities needed for the profession, I just needed the training. The thought of a possible aviation career sustained me for the time being, but fate had other plans.

WORK

With school over I had two years before my apprenticeship was to start, so I had time to go out and earn some money. This sounds as if an apprentice didn't get paid, but that's not quite true. We did get paid – 10 cents per hour, which was a big improvement from olden times when you *paid* to learn a trade.

My first job was at a bank where my main assignment was that of a carrier, making two trips a day to the headquarters in Copenhagen. On these daily train rides into town, I had problems staying awake and would doze off now and again. One time I woke as we stopped at my station and made it out just as the doors closed, but my briefcase didn't. There I stood, on the platform as the train pulled away with the briefcase containing unknown riches. It has never been in my nature to panic, but right then and there I came close. I telephoned the end station and pleaded my case. Enormous relief; it was still there.

As this was during the height of the war some of those excursions to Copenhagen could be quite exciting, like on August 29, 1943, when the Germans introduced martial law. Fully armed German soldiers were stationed at every intersection where they interrogated every pedestrian as to identity, where they came from, where they were going, and why – tremendous excitement for a youngster like me.

Another assignment on this job was to report the daily stock market results which I received by telephone from the main branch. I then wrote them on a tablet, and posted it outside the main entrance door – really quite a nice job.

A FORTUNATE CHANCE MEETING

For some obscure reason I decided to take a course at night school, in typing no less. I have no idea what inspired me to do that. How could I have known, at the age of fourteen, that in the distant future I would be spending endless hours behind a computer? As it were, this turned out to be one of those decisions that change the course of your life. One of my class mates told me about a fellow in another class by the name of Eli Nielsen who also built model gliders, and it was arranged for us to meet in the hallway during recess. Thus began a friendship which is still alive and well after 67 years despite having been half a world apart since 1948. We have visited each other a few times and are in contact by phone on a regular bases, reminiscing about the old days and keeping up with new developments in our respective worlds. Nowadays, I ring him up whenever I am in need of another sustaining infusion of Danish humor.

It did not take long for us to team up our model building in the workshop at the apartment building.

Then we got the idea of starting a model airplane club, and rented a basement downtown. This became fairly successful. During the winter months the basement was heated with a coal burning stove. The problem was however that during the war coal was hard to find, unless your dad just happened to be the superintendent of a apartment complex that was centrally heated by coal burning furnaces. It wasn't too difficult for me to lay my hands on the necessary supply. So on our meeting nights I would show up with a cardboard box under my arm containing the precious merchandise. This was no trivial undertaking as it was quite a walk to get there. But it made me an instant hero.

It did not take long for the club to undertake another more exciting venture. Eli, being two years older than I, had joined the Danish resistance. From time to time he would bring in piles of underground newspapers for distribution. Fortunately we never got caught.

Then a fellow by the name of Arne Olsen joined the club, and Eli, Arne and I became a close threesome. If we were not at the club, we were building models at the workshop in our apartment building basement.

INVENTING THE STATIONARY BIKE

The models we built were made from scratch. The wing ribs and the bulkheads for the fuselage were cut out of 1 mm plywood which we could afford to buy. The longerons, the longitudinal thin strips supporting the ribs and bulkheads in the fuselage, were a little too expensive.

We desperately needed a circular saw to make our own parts, so what to do? There was only one option – build one. The first major obstacle was that we didn't know how to lay our hands on a motor, but we solved that problem rather ingeniously we thought. Somewhere we scrounged up an old bicycle frame which we mounted on a table, and the saw blade shaft was fitted with a sprocket which was driven by a chain from the bicycle. One of us would sit on the bicycle frame, peddling vigorously while another would be doing the cutting. This arrangement actually worked quite satisfactorily as long as the one doing the cutting was not in a hurry. The wood had to be fed through the saw rather gently so as not to exhaust the guy doing the peddling. We didn't realize it, but we had just invented the stationary bike.

This story is not my imagination running away with me; in May of 2010, I called Arne, whom I had not been in contact with since leaving Denmark. He was thrilled to hear from me, and the very first thing he said was: "Do you remember the table saw we built, powered by a bicycle? – those were the days!"

By this time our model building enterprise had outgrown our tiny basement cubicle. Fortunately, as superintendent for the apartment complex my dad had his own good size workshop which he was willing to share.

Sometime around this time, the three of us took up dancing lessons. We learned the foxtrot, quickstep, tango and more. This was a cultural thing; in Denmark at that time, learning to dance and attending dancing classes was sort of mandatory. Oddly enough, we seemed to enjoy it just the same – the girls might have had something to do with that.

THE JOB FROM HELL

I am not sure what inspired me to quit the bank job. It might have been money or rather the lack of it.

However, my next experience in the working world was not a happy one. During the war there was no gasoline available; the Germans needed all of it for their war machine. All private vehicles were powered by gas that was generated by a small stove, burning two-inch sized wood cubes.

The process of cutting these cubes naturally produced an enormous amount of saw dust. This saw dust was to be shoveled into a wooden enclosure with a screen at the front and a vacuum pipe at the back. As a junior laborer, this was my job. The sawing operation worked three shifts but I only worked one 8 hour shift. The net result was that when I got there in the morning, the vacuum box was so full that it was buried beneath an 8 foot high mound of saw dust. First I had to uncover the box, which took about half the day, and the other half was spent shoveling the saw dust into the vacuum box. Needless to say, I did not look forward to going to work in the morning.

Fortunately my dad managed to get me started in the apprenticeship program ahead of schedule.

ENTERING THE WORLD OF GLIDING

By now I was really getting obsessed with the idea of getting airborne. As my kites were progressively getting bigger I got the brilliant idea that tying enough of them together in a row with a chair suspended from the last kite would be a neat method of getting off the ground. I was considerably proud of this invention, not knowing it had already been done.

Around this same time, in spite of my obsession with flying, I felt drawn to the sea - which must have been my Viking blood - and joined a rowing club. For a brief period I tried my hand at sculling. Then Eli picked up some information which not only ended my brief sculling career, but changed my life forever: the existence of a gliding club, Birkerød Svæveflyve Klub (Birkerød Gliding Club), in a little town by the name of Birkerød about 12 km from where we lived. The excitement was overpowering; imagine, real gliders – off we went to check it out.

At that time I had yet to see a picture of a glider, never mind a real one. This was in the early spring of 1944. Unfortunately, the chance to see a glider had to wait; they didn't have one, but were in full swing of building an SG-38. The SG-38 was a single seat, open primary (no enclosed fuselage), the most popular trainer at the time. The wing span was 10.4 meter and the net weight 220 lbs.

Without hesitation Eli, Arne, and I joined. As was to be expected it was no small task to convince my parents that this was a perfectly safe and reasonable venture to pursue, but fortunately I succeeded.

The club had been in existence for only one year and consisted of twelve members. I think the average age was no more than twenty and the "old timer" was probably in his thirty's. The glider was expected to be completed in six months. Heck, six months of duty in the shop seemed a small price to pay for the chance to actually experience flight. The mere thought of it was intoxicating.

WOOD POWERED WINCH

Of course the glider would not be of much use without a means to launch it.

To satisfy that need the club purchased an old Nash truck and a Studebaker sedan from an automobile wrecker. Transmogrifying these two old wrecks into winches turned out to be another momentous task. At this point in time I have no idea why we needed two. Perhaps we thought a spare may come in handy.

The Nash went through a major redesign. Since gasoline was a rare commodity, the first task was to incorporate a wood gas generator. This was a common modification to trucks and cars during the war. Every vehicle was equipped with a gas generator of which the main component was a wood burning stove. The wire drum, guide and cutter were mounted sideways on a structure at the rear in a 90° angle to the direction of travel of the truck. This required an extended drive shaft to drive the drum. Once the winch had been driven to the place of operation, the regular drive shaft was replaced by the longer version to make the drum turn.

A simpler approach was used on the Studebaker. Here the drum was simply mounted to one of the rear wheels and the wire guide and cutter was mounted on the front bumper. Strangely, a wood gas generator was not installed on the Studebaker. I have no idea where we thought we would get the gasoline from.

The momentous task of building these winches was made possible by one ingenious, hardworking member of the club by the name of Christian Lund who seemingly possessed the ability to accomplish the impossible. No doubt being an automobile mechanic by trade had something to do with it.

Of course other members participated in the construction as well, but when it came to winches, Christian was the driving force.

ACCOMPLISHING SO MUCH WITH SO LITTLE

The Birkenrød Gliding Club's workshop was a rented old garage that we heated with a homemade stove, fueled by used motor oil drippings onto a bunch of rags. To adjust the temperature we simply adjusted the flow of oil. We didn't consider ourselves as being poor; we just didn't have any money. Consequently, everything had to be built from scratch.

Another minor problem which had to be solved was that none of us knew anything about building gliders, but somehow we managed to get guidance and instruction from other clubs.

That first glider was ready to fly by September of that year, 1944, three months ahead of schedule, and one of the winches was completed as well.

In addition to thousands of man hours, the primary glider cost us the not so small fortune of $400 in material and the necessary tools. Raising the required capital was a constant struggle, but there was no limit to our resourcefulness. At one time we fabricated and sold children's pushcarts for $2 each. We also acquired discarded lawnmowers from a scrap dealer which we rebuilt, sharpened, painted and sold for $1 each. As you might guess, those efforts didn't quite manage to raise the necessary cash. We ultimately had to take more drastic measures to raise money. No sooner had we completed the first SG-38 when we started building a second one for the purpose of selling it. As if that wasn't enough, we took out a loan to purchase some parts for a Grunau Baby from another club and started that project as well.

In the club's first two and a half years, three gliders and two winches were completed. Thinking back on it now, how so few of us managed to accomplish so much in such a short time, is beyond me. Of course building gliders was not all we had to do, we also had jobs to attend to.

The apprenticeship program I was enlisted in included night school during the winter months, five days a week from 6 to 8 PM. Becoming a toolmaker was no trivial matter and night school included subjects such as math, metallurgy, drafting, geometry, etc. In those days, if the machine you were building required a gear, you had to make it yourself, and setting up the gear cutter required a hefty application of geometry. Nowadays a gear is simply a purchased item.

My daily schedule was to work from 8 a.m.to 4:30 p.m., followed by evening classes from 6 to 8 p.m., then back on the bicycle and out to work in the shop till about 11 p.m. My specialty became to make wing ribs.

Where in the world did we get all that vigor? The vitality of youth plus boundless enthusiasm I suppose. Yet, it doesn't even seem possible, but honestly I am not making it up. All this has been well documented and is not just drawn from my memory entirely. No wonder I don't have much energy left.

We didn't appreciate it at the time, but because of our frenzied quest to fly we escaped a serious mental condition which inflicts many youths of the present generation – boredom.

FUN AND PARTIES

Now I wouldn't want you to think it was all work and no play; we did squeeze in some time for the occasional practical joke and a party now and then. In the winter months we would spend Saturday nights in the shop. Preparing to bed down around midnight, totally exhausted, you just might discover that the comfort of your sleeping bag had been enhanced by a generous application of wood shavings.

Parties; this is one art form in which the Danes excel. They know how to dance, sing, and have a few drinks in between. At one party I felt the need for a little nap before heading home. I woke up at 7 in the morning, looked at the clock and exclaimed with some distress, "And I should have been home at eleven." When I got home I hesitantly walked in the door as my parents were having breakfast not knowing what kind of greeting to expect. They simply asked if I had had a good time. Only later did I find out they had been worried sick and envisioned me having fallen off my bicycle and laying in a ditch somewhere, bleeding to death.

During our Saturday over-night-stays at the shop the most delightful experience was breakfast. Early morning, a couple of us would be assigned on a mission to the local bakery to purchase a couple of bags of fresh pastry, several loaves of warm French bread, and a pound of butter. This scrumptious, nourishing breakfast sustained us for the rest of the weekend; there was no need for lunch or dinner. To fully understand why I am talking about this, it is necessary for the reader to have experienced Danish baking first hand. It is difficult to describe, but here is one attempt at it. Taking a morning walk along Main Street in any Danish town, before you get out of range of the mouth watering aroma from the bakery you just passed, you will no doubt pick up the scent from the next one down the street. And they are as good as they were plentiful.

OTHER OBSTACLES

Perhaps I should mention that I was expected to do other things in my free time than just build gliders.

The apartment complex that my dad looked after was heated by three large coal burning furnaces. The coal was loaded through a 12 inch door at the top of each furnace. The coal was brought to the furnaces in a conical shaped container, suspended from a trolley which rode on a track above the furnaces, and dumped into the coal bin where it was reloaded by shovel. I often helped with that task, mostly when my parents were out. Keeping the furnaces from starving was not that big of a chore until the coal supply dried up. When that happened the first substitute was blocks of peat. This made the job considerably more time consuming, but nothing compared to what we were faced with near the end of the war when we ran out of peat – tree stumps.

Huge mountains of massive tree stumps had to be reduced to pieces that could fit through the 12 inch doors. This was accomplished with sledge hammers, numerous wedges, and hand saws – a Herculean task. My uncle from Copenhagen joined forces, and between the three of us we succeeded. Without a doubt, after a few weeks of this routine we could have entered any lumberjack competition and secured an easy win. The next challenge was to get these scraps of wood loaded into the furnaces – those details escaped my memory. However, there were two things in our favor; providing hot running water to the apartments and exceeding a room temperature of 64.5° F was strictly forbidden. Also, we were tremendously lucky we did not enter this state of affairs until late winter 1944. The war ended May 4th, 1945, bringing this era to an end, but it was long enough. I do not recall what we used for fuel the coming winter, but it was not wood – I would have remembered that.

There were further obligations that imposed on my precious time. Two of the apartment buildings were parallel to each other with a huge lawn in between. Naturally I had to do my share of the lawn cutting. This was no easy task as we used a "push" mower. This was a "push" mower in the strictest sense – no motor.

To ease our food shortage during the war the occupants of each apartment were allocated a garden plot for the purpose of growing vegetables. Our garden plot, which we maintained for two years, was located at the end of our street about half a mile from the apartment. My job was to bring water to the plot. This was accomplished by using a yoke placed on my shoulders with a bucket of water suspended from each end. Needless to say, one watering session required numerous trips.

LOOPING AN SG-38

September 4, 1944, was the big day, as our pride and joy was to be test flown. It turned out to be quiet a spectacle. The test pilot, one of the instructors, felt obligated to execute a loop to adequately establish airworthiness. To have a reasonable chance at getting over the top, the loop had to be initiated with a nearly vertical dive with the wind screaming through the wires, and then he barely flopped over the top. Our workmanship must have been up to standard as all went well. We didn't even loose the "T" wrench used for tightening the guide wires, which we had forgotten to remove from the top of the fuselage after rigging; it was still in place after he landed. I didn't realize it at the time, but this was a once in a lifetime experience. I am not likely to witness that stunt again.

He was the same intrepid pilot who sometime later rewarded a 12 year old kid who had been helping out with the operation with a ride in (I suppose it should be *on*) the primary. The instructor accomplished this by simply having the boy sit on his knee, holding onto him with one arm while he flew with the other.

Then another problem surfaced; none of us knew anything about flying. Again we had to seek help from outside sources. During that first short season two instructors from other clubs, sympathetic to our plight, came to our rescue.

It's noteworthy to observe that throughout the war the German Occupying Forces permitted us to fly, although with a 600ft height restriction which, it is now safe to admit was not strictly adhered to.

FLYING, AT LAST

During the first few launches we didn't even get off the ground; they were mere ground slides for the purpose of teaching us how to keep the wings level.

The following Sunday was to be the day we had been waiting for – we were to get airborne. We stayed over-night in the shop the day before. My vocabulary is far too limited to fully describe the suspense and excitement we experienced that night. Needless to say, none of us slept much. Although we couldn't expect to get much over 6 feet off the ground, we would be flying. The concept of that was overpowering. Just imagine, at 15 years old I would finally realize my life's dream!

And yes, we did get to fly. The flights were brief, but thrilling. The instructor showed us the position in which to hold the stick. We were to move it only side to side to keep the wings level, but under no circumstance were we to move it fore or aft. Our height would be controlled by the winch driver. Just think; it only took six month of work to reach this goal.

During the following Sundays, each flight got progressively higher and longer. At twenty five feet or so we had to release the cable, maintain airspeed and flare. After 20 flights or so, with the last few reaching a couple hundred feet and included a few, more or less controlled "S" turns, we were to graduate to a full 800 ft. launch. For me, unfortunately, this milestone had to wait till the following year.

This was the time I got the best instructional advice I have ever received. My instructor told us, "There are three things you must always remember, and they are: speed, speed and speed." Even with today's emphasis on low energy landings, I still feel more comfortable with a few extra knots in the pattern, and it seems to have served me well.

We are not all born to fly. When we arrived at the stage where we practiced 'S' turns one of the "elder" members had trouble getting the hang of it, and you could hear him hollering, "Turn you devil, turn you devil." – she didn't listen.

THE SG-38

I think a few facts regarding the SG-38 primary trainer are in order.

During the twenties there were several primary designs in use in Germany for pilots learning to fly the hard way (solo). They tended to be very light and fragile. One design had the fuselage tower strut in front of the pilot. This soon gave this glider the nickname "skull splitter".

Then in 1938 Edmund Schneider who lived in the town of Grunau, with the help of two others, developed the SG-38. They set out to design a primary that would a) be easy and gentle to fly, b) easy and as cheap as possible to build and repair, and c) strong and as safe as possible in case of a crash. When you look at an SG-38, strong and safe are two adjectives which do not readily spring to mind. Nonetheless it has proven to be a very successful trainer and yes, reasonably safe.

The number of SG-38's built is somewhere between 7,000 and 8,000, making it one of the most popular gliders ever produced.

Performance-wise, the glide ratio was 8/1 at 30 mph, at a sink rate of 6 ft. per second. This would equate to 2 minutes of flying time from an 800 ft. tow, and that's what we got. Contrary to common belief, the name SG does not stand for "Schulgleiter", but for the manufacturer "Schneider Grunau", and "38" marks the year of its design.

WAR STORIES

The first airfield we flew from, we shared with the Germans. We operated on one side and the Hitlerjüngen on the other. They seemed to have had an abundance of everything. When they broke a glider, they simply went into the hangar and got another one.

We were in desperate need of a new winch cable and surely the Germans would have a spare reel of new wire handy. After some reconnoitering we identified the location of their supply depot, or so we thought. This was exciting. If Eli, Arne, and I could pull this off we would surely be treated as heroes.

On a moonless night, operation "Winch Cable" was set into motion. Stealthily we crept toward our target. Within a couple of hundred feet we stopped and laid still for a while – all was quiet. We made our move and found the supply depot. After groping around in the dark for a while, it was with much elation we got our hands on a reel of wire. Conveyance of our loot was a challenge, crawling through fields pushing this monstrous reel with some 3,000 ft of steel cable ahead of us, but we prevailed.

Later, when we managed to properly evaluate our stolen treasure we made a most discouraging discovery; it wasn't the supply depot we had plundered, but the scrap heap – super hero status was not to be.

One of the advantages of the hectic schedule we maintained was that I slept well.

The front door to the apartment building had a full size glass pane. One morning as I was leaving for work, the glass pane was shattered. Must have been the milkman I thought, but I couldn't help but notice the pile of glass on the floor was out of proportion to the size of the door. Looking up the stairwell I discovered the glass in the windows on all three floors was missing. I was puzzled. It wasn't till I got to work that I learned from my coworkers that a factory located practically next door to our apartment building was blown up by saboteurs. They couldn't believe I slept through it. There were even bits of shrapnel in the walls of the apartment building here and there.

So, sleeping like a rock, how did I manage to get up in time in the morning? Very simple, my dad grabbed my legs and pulled me onto the floor. Amazingly, such drastic measures were not necessary on Sundays when it was time to go flying.

THE ULTIMATE DREAM

At our age, we had a lively imagination. The ultimate dream was to somehow get to England and fly Spitfires.

Before we left we would have our "A" badge pin, a small round medallion with one seagull on a blue background, made into a finger ring. Here is the neat part; when we crashed and burned, which we were sure to do sooner or later, the investigating team would rummaged through the ashes, find the ring, and exclaim with deep admiration: "Ah, he was a *glider pilot*" – such dreams.

THIRD REICH TO THE RESCUE, AGAIN

As we neared the completion of the Grunau Baby we faced another problem. Contrary to the primary which did not require any instruments, the Grunau Baby, being an "advanced" glider, did. Now, where could we possibly get such things as an altimeter, airspeed indicator, and variometer? Again, the only possible source was the Third Reich. Several volunteers accepted the challenge.

I never did learn the details of that expedition, but it was more fruitful than our winch cable mission. I think it was a static exhibit put on by the Luftwaffe. Our team came prepared with the appropriate tools and left with their pockets full containing the required merchandise. One thing I want to make clear; this was not pilfering. By relieving the Germans of a few instruments we were in fact supporting a noble cause.

MYSTERIOUS PHONE CALL

Somewhere around this time I almost lost my best friend Eli. Fortunately his family's house was not equipped with the luxury of in-house plumbing, which very likely saved his life. He was a member of the resistance movement and one day, as he was responding to nature's call, he heard the Gestapo stomping up the garden path to the house to arrest him. He escaped by running out the back and across the fields. I knew nothing of this.

Then one evening I received a mysterious phone call: "Meet me under the 'so and so' bridge tonight at 8 o'clock," click. No name given, but of course I knew who it was. I made my appearance at the exact time at the specified point of rendezvous, and sure enough there he was. In an effort to conceal himself he had his coat collar pulled up over his ears, and his hat pulled down over his eyes which were obscured by sun glasses – obviously a consequence of watching too many Hollywood movies. It is a miracle he didn't get arrested just on the grounds of looking suspicious.

Two weeks later the underground arranged for his passage to Sweden where he joined the Danish brigade. The Danish brigade, a group of young Danes who escaped the German occupation by making their way to Sweden, received extensive military training by, also escaped, Danish officers. The size of the brigade ultimately reached 6,000 men and women. The aim was to assist in the liberation of Denmark if it came to fighting, possibly in combination with an allied invasion. For so many Jews and resistance fighters to have successfully crossed the sea to Sweden, it seems hard not to believe that none of the German patrols looked the other way.

MORE EXCITEMENT

On March 21, 1945, we had a bit of excitement. I was at work operating a lathe, positioned in front of a window, when I happened to spot an aircraft in the distance, approaching at only a few hundred feet above the ground. On closer inspection we determined it was a RAF Mosquito, a light bomber, and it was heading straight at us – we were thrilled.

We all ran out and waved enthusiastically as he went straight overhead. In retrospect this wasn't really that clever. Some of the machine tools we build could have been destined for Germany, and we could well have been the target. As it were, he was one of a group RAF pilots returning from a highly successful raid on the Gestapo headquarters in Copenhagen.

The Gestapo had obtained detailed knowledge on the activities of the Danish resistance movement which was becoming more effective in hampering the German operations, and it became necessary for the resistance to have this information – and preferably also the Gestapo people – eliminated.

The Gestapo had taken over a large building in Copenhagen and set up offices on the lower floors. To discourage any bombing of this building, they housed prisoners on the upper level. The RAF faced a considerable challenge when diving down in the street, approach the building and aim their bombs for the bottom floor while in a steep turn to get out of there. The attack was a success to the extent that a number of prisoners who were held in the building for interrogation managed to escape. Unfortunately on the way out one of the planes struck a flagpole and crashed into a school killing 114 children.

THE END OF THE WAR

On May 4, 1945, Arne and I were downstairs in our apartment basement workshop working on our models and as usual listening to the Danish BBC radio broadcast from England, when we heard the most profound announcement of our lifetime: "The Germans have capitulated" – the war was over. We wasted no time getting out of the basement. Immediately the streets were crowded with jubilant people. The blackout curtains were torn down and burned in the streets and being replaced with candles in the windows. We ultimately wound up in the middle of a huge crowd on the city square in Copenhagen where one of our then famous actors climbed the town hall tower, and sang a song which lyrics that roughly translated were something like: "When we get a boat with bananas there will be summer and sunshine again". Composed and written especially for the occasion – the spirit of the crowd was electrifying. But that boat with bananas was a long time in coming. It took a few years before the availability of such commodities returned to pre-war status.

Officially the capitulation was effective May 5, at 8 a.m. What we did not realize at the time was that this only applied to Holland, Denmark and north-west Germany. Regrettably there were still more battles that would take place in southern Germany which destroyed more lives than were lost on D-Day.

For me, the horrific brutalities of war didn't really register until the war was over and we saw the first film footage of the death camps as the prisoners were liberated. In the local movie theaters, news real was shown before the feature movie. Seeing those hapless human victims, nothing but skeletons with skin stretched over their bones, was horrifying. Human nature has it flaws. Too bad we didn't evolve from the gentle gorillas instead of from the aggressive, war-minded chimpanzees; maybe the world would have been a better place.

Now, realizing that millions of people had suffered unimaginable, inhumane atrocities, while I had the time of my life, I almost developed a guilt complex. It did not, then or now, seem fair.

There was one uplifting event that took place after the war that needs to be mentioned. The Danish people welcomed home the Jewish people that survived the concentration camps and the ones that returned from Sweden by offering them a clean house with fresh flowers in a vase, compliments of their Christian neighbors.

GLIDER CAMP

Later that summer of 1945 we organized our first glider camp, a joint venture with a much bigger club. This was not a competition, but simply a get together for a week of gliding. The place was the airfield of Bøtø, at the very southern tip of Denmark.

To convince my parents to part with the necessary cash to fund this expedition was no small feat, but I finally wore them down and they relented. Not that it was all that expensive. All the flying was included in our monthly dues, and we slept and ate in a barn. The food was plentiful, but basic.

At that time we had 12 members in our club and 11 of us went to the camp. We didn't realize it then, but we lived in a unique society. This would not have been possible in the United States; eleven young people, most of us in the working, being able to take a one week vacation all at the same time – impossible. In Denmark, by law every working person got four weeks' vacation a year, no matter what. This has since been increased to five weeks.

Now we were faced with one minor problem; how to transport our gliders (by this time the Grunau Baby had been completed) and our winches the 100 or so miles to our destination – we had no trailers for the gliders. But there was no end to our resourcefulness. The gliders and the Studebaker were shipped by train and the Nash winch was driven. The fellows driving the Nash had more fun than they bargained for. The tires were in bad shape as replacements had not been available for the past six years. They had 19 flats along the way.

When it came to obtaining gasoline for the Studebaker, we had more luck. During the war the airfield where the camp was held had been used by the Luftwaffe, and there were still some wrecked airplanes left, among them a few Ju-52's. Fortunately there was enough gas left in the tanks to sustain the Studebaker for the week.

During this camp I got my first 800 ft launch. I have lived a long time and have forgotten a lot of things, but I won't live long enough to forget that first pattern. That event is engraved in my memory as if it happened last week. I can vividly see the winch between my feet during the launch. Then after release, my instructor John Wetlesen, standing in the middle of the field guiding me around the pattern by signaling with a flag when to turn. My mind has no trouble reconstructing the sensations experienced on that first 90° turn. For someone who had never been above 200 ft before, it was the thrill of a lifetime.

Aside from getting the grandfather of all sunburns, this gliding camp adventure was definitely one of the high points in my life – nothing but gliding for a whole week.

This is where I met Harold Jensen, at that time known only as Cowboy perhaps because he always wore cowboy boots or maybe because of his free spirit. After the camp, the next time I saw Harold was at the U.S. Nationals in 1959. He was wearing overalls, leaning against his Lo-150 on the take-off grid. I walked up to him and said "Don't you ever clean that thing?" referring to the glider. Without hesitation he took the can of beer he had standing on the wing, dribbled some along the leading edge, and gave it a little rub with his elbow, "How is that?" – that was Harold.

One noteworthy statistic from this camp is that we made 745 launches without one single accident.

FIRST CLUB INSTRUCTOR

The following year an instructor by the name of Anton Carlsen joined the club and we became self-reliant. Incidentally, sea captain Carlsen who gained world fame sometime in the early sixties for his refusal to abandon his sinking freighter was his brother. Then in August of 1946 the president of our club went to Sweden and obtained his glider instructor certificate.

FIB EXPOSED

My mother wasn't exactly thrilled about this flying business. As a matter of fact, she was worried sick, but I managed to put her mind somewhat at ease by explaining that nothing could happen because if anything went wrong we would simply let go of the controls and the glider would float to the ground gently like a feather. None of us imagined that someday, some people would consider gliding a dangerous sport.

That worked well enough until my well-intended fib was disclosed at a party, attended by my mother. Our instructor Anton Carlsen felt obligated to make a speech in which he confessed that he was a complete nervous wreck every single time he sent one of us aloft. I must admit, if I had to instruct 15 and 16 year olds by standing on the ground guiding them around the pattern by pointing a flag, I would be a nervous wreck as well.

My mother consoled herself in her belief that this flying nonsense was just a passing fancy anyway which I would surely abandon before long. She held firm to that conviction until the end of her life at the age of 91. Of course she might still be proven right; I just haven't grown up yet. Anyways, there is no sign of this happening anytime soon. Whenever I drive to the glider field and the weather looks promising, I am as excited as a kid the day before Christmas. On the other hand, a deserted, forlorn looking contest site emptied of all the gliders and trailers after a contest makes me feel like a kid the day *after* Christmas.

OUR FIRST AIRLINE FLIGHT

After my buddy Eli returned from Sweden we thought it would be exciting to try an airline flight. So we went to the SAS ticket office in Copenhagen and inquired about booking a flight, we didn't care where it went, we just wanted the cheapest. This turned out to be a round trip flight to Malmø, Sweden.

I have forgotten the price, but the duration of the flight was 20 minutes. The airplane was a Ford Trimotor, which accommodated up to 8 passengers. All surfaces were covered with corrugated sheet metal, and it cruised at the amazing speed of 145 km (90 miles) per hour. It was one of the first airplanes designed for air travel that had the luxury of an enclosed cabin. We had a marvelous time. In Malmø we had just enough time to visit some distant family of mine who treated us to our first piece of chocolate in 6 years.

Nonetheless, we did have a bid of bad luck. The following week on the same flight the Trimotor lost one of its wheels. To minimize the risk of fire upon landing, the pilot circled above their destination for an addition two hours to burn off excessive fuel. Now, why couldn't we have been on that flight! Just one week later and we could have enjoyed all that extra time in the air.

THRILLS

Flying a primary, sitting in the open air was great fun and added some thrills we don't get to enjoy anymore. The seat was simply a flat piece of plywood so if you had failed to tighten your seat belt, an uncoordinated turn was rewarded with a breathtaking sensation as you slid toward the edge of the seat. Incidentally, we had not yet been introduced to the term "coordinated turn", we were simply instructed to apply rudder and aileron at the same time. Even the Grunau didn't have a bank indicator, and the slip string hadn't been invented yet.

After the "B" certificate, which was awarded after twenty complete patterns in the primary, we transitioned to the Grunau. After flying the primary, graduating to the Grunau was a real treat.

MY FIRST THERMAL

The next momentous event was my first thermal, which, of course, was in the Grunau Baby. It must have been the mother lode of all thermals because in spite of my gross mishandling of the controls (I barely managed to keep the thing right side up), I topped off at 3,000' with the vistas of Copenhagen spread out below me. For us, there had never been any doubt that flying would be awesome and thrilling, but we never dreamt it could be anything as spectacular as this. That flight earned me the "C" certificate and I felt as if I had joined some elite brotherhood of adventurers.

HITTING THE ROAD

We were an enthusiastic lot; virtually nothing could keep us grounded. One season we did not have access to an airfield, but we were determined not to let anything deter us from our quest to fly. Every Sunday we loaded our primary onto a borrowed truck, and with a bunch of us standing in the back holding on to the de-rigged primary, we headed out on the country roads with winch and all. Those of us who could not find room on the vehicles were towed behind on their bicycles hanging on to a rope. Quite a procession. When we spotted a suitable field we would ask the farmer if he would mind if we made a few tows. Perhaps this is the reason why off-airport landings never were such a traumatic experience for me – I was raised on off-airport take-off and landings.

There were times when we couldn't find a field long enough and we had to resort to using a couple of adjoining fields. On one location the winch cable had to cross two barbed wire fences, but that worked well enough, it even added another element of excitement. From time to time the cable would get snagged on one of the fences, and we were treated to a moment of suspense wondering if the cable would come unstuck or take the fence with it. Amazingly, we never pulled out a fence, and when the angle of the cable got steep enough it would come unstuck with a 'twang'. At another location the winch could not be seen from the launch point because of the hilly terrain, and a relay signaler had to be placed somewhere in the middle.

It was definitely a cumbersome and time consuming mode of operation, having to pack up everything and tour the countryside looking for a field every Sunday. Luckily we soon found a farmer who took a liking to us and let us use his field as a permanent base the rest of the season after the hay had been harvested. He also let us store the de-rigged primary in his barn. Then, to make sure we were well nourished, he brought a large can of milk to the launch site. By the way, we only flew on Sundays as most of us had to work on Saturdays.

One day our benevolent farmer, seeing the struggle we endured retrieving the winch cable, expressed the thought that a horse would be more suitable and lent us one. This arrangement worked just fine until the hour came of the horse's scheduled feeding. With total disregard for all our coaching and pleading it strode resolutely and serenely back to the barn to enjoy its customary meal. Unfortunately it had dragged the attached cable with it all the way into the barn.

RAINY DAYS WERE THE BEST

Gliding was 1% flying and 99% work, some of which was in the category of hard labor such as the retrieval of the winch cable by hand. To expedite this process we organized two, three-man teams. By the time one team arrived at the launch site with the end of the cable, the other was back at the winch ready to walk out the cable after the next drop. In spite of this efficient operation you might slave a whole Sunday and not get to fly, but whenever that happened you would be at the front of the line the following Sunday.

There were numerous potential problems which might impede operations such as excessive cable breaks, winch problems, etc. Then of course, every landing was not perfectly smooth and at times the glider would be out of commission until after it had received some special attention in the shop.

But rainy days were the best, as not all the members would show up and making several flights was a real possibility. Gliding was indeed a physical sport.

We typically left home for the airfield at 6 a.m. and didn't return till late in the evening, totally exhausted and barely able to get off our bicycles.

OTHER AMUSEMENTS

Occasionally the three of us would take a break and engage in something less constructive. Those sessions would inexplicably coincide with the evenings my parents weren't home. We would do wild things like play cards while listening to our records (those were 78 RPM records, as the long play version had yet to be invented). Naturally our choice of music was pretty wild including tunes like "Roll out the Barrel," "Our Home Town Mountain Band," and such.

The machine we played those records on was not exactly "state-of-the-art". The turntable was not electrically powered, but driven by a spring which had to be wound by hand. To make matters worse, this gramophone had some years on it and the spring had weakened to the point where it had to be wound almost continuously. A further inconvenience was that the needle had to be changed for every record, and a record only played for 3 minutes. This obviously impeded our card game to some extent. Nonetheless we had a marvelous time. Not long thereafter, needles became available that were good for ten records – pure luxury.

MY FIRST PARTNERSHIP IN A GLIDER

In 1947, we operated off an airfield where one of the gliders, a Grunau Baby, was owned by a partnership of three glider pilots. We were very much impressed. This was obviously the way to go; they could stay up for as long as they could or liked, not limited to half hour flights dictated by club rules. Now that it looked like we might eventually learn to extend our flights beyond flying mere patterns, the thought of having to terminate a flight on purpose was unbearable. The decision was made, and the three of us plus our instructor Anton Carlsen started to build a Grunau Baby. This was my first part ownership in a glider. The project was started in our apartment building basement workshop.

THOSE WERE THE DAYS

Those were truly great days. The sense of accomplishment, the camaraderie, the parties, the thrill of adventure, and a feel of belonging. Many friendships were forged that lasted a lifetime. We were almost like a family. Sad to say, there are now only four of us left from that era.

Now I realize how extremely lucky I was to have entered the world of gliding before the end of the solo training – primary – era, or I would have missed the most exhilarating days of my love affair with soaring. It was actually quite safe, and none of us sustained any injuries, but we did spend some time in the shop working on repairs.

We didn't realize it at the time, but we accomplished much more that merely building gliders and winches. We created fabulous memories which have sustained me through life – what a grand time we had.

THE DRAW OF THE WILD WEST

In 1948, the Danes were still plagued by limited supplies of just about everything. My dad had a brother in Canada who painted a rosy picture of life over there. He had a laundry in a town called Whitehorse, in the Yukon Territory, and supposedly one in Dawson City. He proposed that if we were to join him, he would make my dad a business partner and my dad could operate the laundry in Dawson City. As it turned out the entire scheme was a fairy tale. As a matter of fact, Dawson City was a desolate ghost town. Why my uncle and aunt were so keen on luring us over there is beyond me, especially since my aunt came over for a visit after the war and was able to witness our living conditions. Sure there were many items which were in short supply, but we still lived comfortably in a civilized and technically advanced society with such luxuries as running water and inside toilets, a far cry from what awaited us in the Yukon. Regrettably, my dad saw this as a business opportunity and accepted the invitation. As it turned out, this was a mistake of immense consequences.

THE HARDEST THING I EVER DID

Leaving Demark was the hardest thing I have ever had to do. I had not finished my apprenticeship program. The company I was employed with strongly advised my parents to let me stay behind to graduate, but they just could not bring themselves to leaving me behind. Now I ponder if they had let me remain to finish my apprenticeship, would I have ever left Denmark? – probably not.

Saying goodbye to gliding and all my friends was almost more than I could bear. I consoled myself with the thought that perhaps gliding might be further advanced in Canada – what a pipe dream that was.

Nonetheless, on the 20th of March 1948, my mother and I (my dad having left a couple of months earlier) boarded an American Overseas Airlines' four piston engines driven DC-6 and left Denmark for the land of plenty, lured by the promise of riches – I reluctantly left my 25% share of a perfectly good set of wing ribs for a Grunau Baby behind.

Working on the SG-38

Luxurious toilet facilities

Trial rigging and inspection

Crowded shop

A trip to the lumber yard

Transmogrifying this heap of junk into a winch was obviously impossible – but we didn't know that.

Thus was every taxi in Copenhagen outfitted during the war – note the bags of wood on top.

Me – 1945

Eli Nielsen – August 1945

Arne Olsen – August 1945

65 Years later, 2010 – from left: Eli, Arne and me.

The Nash being driven out to the launching point. The creator, Christian Lund, on the running board.

The more primitive Studebaker. Note, the motorcycle for retrieving the cable – pure luxury.

Retrieving the cable -- half a mile to go

Nice launch -- worth every ounce of toil

On top of the world

Trial rigging of the Grunau Baby IIA -- no spoilers

In 1946, graduating to 'High Performance'.
After the SG-38, anything was high performance.

Horsing around. Me in the Grunau, Eli pestering
me. My cousin Ellen from Canada on the right.

Danish Gliding License

Joined some elite brotherhood of adventurers

6,150 hours, 146,000 miles and 66 years later

Chapter 3

THREE YEARS IN THE YUKON

Throughout my childhood I listened to stories about my uncle, my father's brother, who lived in Canada, and who was talked about with great reverence around my grandparent's dining room table.

My uncle operated a laundry in Whitehorse, Yukon. After the war ended he painted a rosy picture in an attempt to convince my dad to join him in Canada and become his partner operating a second laundry in Dawson City – surely the road to success. My dad felt stuck in his job in Denmark, and having lived through all the shortages during the war, Canada seemed the land of plenty and riches.

My dad left three months earlier to reconnoiter the situation. The idiocy of the venture must have been obvious to him from the start, but coming back would have been seen as a failure and that was unacceptable. And he would not have come back to the way things were before he left; his job was gone, although despite all, the opportunity to make a reasonable living was still much better in Denmark than in the Yukon.

My dad had started many letters telling my mother not to come, that the whole thing had been a terrible mistake, and that he would return as soon as he had enough money for the ticket, but none of them ever got mailed.

AIR TRAVEL ANNO 1948

It was the 20th of March, 1948, three weeks before my 19th birthday. It was a momentous occasion as we were about to leave our country, language, culture, and for me, my gliding and all my gliding friends. I really didn't want to go.

Two aunts, an uncle, and my friend Eli were there to see my mother and me off.

Before we went to the airport we stopped at a restaurant in Copenhagen for Danish pancakes with strawberries and whipped cream. Little did we know it would be years before we would experience such a treat again.

When we arrived at Kastrup Airport, an American Overseas Airline's DC-6, in all its glory, was waiting for us. This being before the time of jet age, it had four piston type engines. There was only one class, and that was "first". Everyone was elegantly dressed – the service was impeccable. There was no catering service, instead meals were prepared on board by a chef and served on the best china along with silver cutlery and crystal glasses.

The Atlantic crossing was routed via Reykjavik, then onto Gander. The estimated flight time was 9 hours 20 minutes to Reykjavik, then 9 hours 30 minutes on to Gander.

Looking at the Danish landscape with its red-tiled roofs as we took off, I wistfully contemplated the possibility that it would be a long time before I would be treated to that sight again. Nonetheless, before long, after having enjoyed a delightful meal topped off with a few glasses of champagne, everyone was in a cheerful mood.

About four and a half hours out of Copenhagen, beyond the point of no return, we encountered a significant front and the cheerful mood quickly evaporated. The DC-6 was not designed to operate at the altitude required to out-climb such massive weather systems, and flying through such monstrous cloud formations is not advisable. The only alternative left was to descend below cloud base. This was indeed exciting; wild turbulence and daunting seascapes. Every lightning strike revealed huge rolling waves barely a few hundred feet below us, inducing somber contemplations. It got even more exciting when we were hit by lightning. All the lights went out, one engine quit, and aside from the feathered propeller we could see a sizable hole in one wing whenever a lightning bolt lit up the scene. Unlike Hollywood's depiction of situations when survival is uncertain, no one ran through the aisle screaming *"we are going to die"*; everyone just sat quietly entrenched in their own thoughts. My mother turned to me and calmly said, "nu tror jeg vi blie'r fiskemad" (I think we are going to be fish food.)

Well, we didn't turn into fish food. We emerged from the storm without further damage, but we had been in even more serious trouble than we realized. The lightning strike had also fried the radios. At that time, the only other means of navigation was the sextant which obviously would not have been of any use. Our flight crew had faced the inconceivable task of finding a distant light in the midst of an ocean of darkness, relying solely on steering a magnetic course based on forecasted winds. No doubt there must have been some tense moments up front, and I can imagine the relief when they spotted those lifesaving lights of a coastline on the horizon. I can't help but ponder how many of today's pilots/navigators would be capable of duplicating such a feat.

In keeping with the times, we were treated to a dinner fit for royalty upon arrival in Reykjavik. We all enjoyed a juicy steak served in an exclusive dining room.

After arranging for a replacement DC-6, the nine and a half hour flight to Gander, Newfoundland was uneventful and much appreciated by all. The rest of the trip to Whitehorse was all by DC-3s, an arduous journey involving numerous stopovers.

A little information on the DC-3. This two engine tail-dragger made its first flight in 1935, had a cruising speed of 150 mph., and accommodated 27 passengers. The seat spacing was more generous than in today's supper stratospheric cruisers and considerably more comfortable. Another feature was cold toilets. Now, I can't be sure all of the DC-3s were equipped in this fashion or if we just got lucky. I discovered the lack of heating in the toilet when over the Canadian Rockies I had to answer a call from Mother Nature; it must have been 20° below zero in there. Unlike the main cabin, the toilet was equipped with a single light switch which allowed me to turn off the light so I could fully appreciate the spectacular views out the porthole. Sitting there in full darkness, the sight of the Rocky Mountains bathing in the magic light of a full moon was pure enchantment. Unfortunately, our old Kodak box camera was safely stored in one of our suitcases, not that it would have even come close to capturing the magic of the moment. Just think; pilots are treated to such splendor from their seats in the cockpit on a regular basis – that's my kind of job! It took some time to tear myself away from the porthole, someone may have wondered if I had frozen to death in there.

To fully appreciate what I am talking about when I say "arduous journey", I need to give you a more detailed account of this trip:

From Gander, Newfoundland, to Sidney, Nova Scotia: flying time 4 hours 20 minutes.

We circled for half an hour over Sydney in a snow storm, at an altitude of about 300ft waiting for the weather to clear. It wasn't long before the constant circling and turbulence started to claim its victims. I think my mother and I were the only ones staying intact, but the sound and smell of it almost claimed us as well. Because the snow persisted, we changed course for an alternative airport, backtracking to Stephenville, Newfoundland.

The rest of the trip didn't offer any noteworthy circumstance other than the number of stops it took to get to our destination:

Stephenville, Newfoundland, to Sidney, Nova Scotia: 1 Hour 10 minutes.
Sidney to Halifax, Nova Scotia, to Moncton, New Brunswick: 2 hours 30 minutes.
Moncton to Montreal, Quebec: 2 hours 45 minutes.
Montreal to Ottawa, Ontario: 45 minutes.
Ottawa to Toronto, Ontario: 1 hour 30 minutes.
Toronto to Sault Ste. Marie to Port Arthur, Ontario, to Winnipeg, Manitoba: 7 hours 10 minutes.
Winnipeg to Saskatoon, Saskatchewan: 2 hours 30 minutes.
Saskatoon to Edmonton, Alberta: 2 hours.

Edmonton to Grande Prairie, Alberta: 1 hour 25 minutes.
Grande Prairie to Ft. St. John, British Columbia: 40 minutes.
Ft. St. John to Fort Nelson, British Columbia: 1 hour 10 minutes.
Fort Nelson to Watson Lake, Yukon, to Whitehorse: 3 hours 25 minutes.

WHITEHORSE

At 10 pm on March 24, 1948, four days and 46 hours of flying time after leaving Copenhagen, we stepped off the airplane at our destination into 24°F below zero temperatures, full of unfounded hope and enthusiasm.

It was just as well we arrived in the dark so all we could see of our new surroundings were the city lights as we drove down the mountain from the airport into town. Had the ramshackle city been revealed to us in its entirety all at once, it might have been too much of a shock.

The first couple of nights we stayed with my aunt and uncle. This allowed us to get our feet on the ground before having to face the total brunt of our situation.

A few days after our arrival we were treated to a ride up the mountain to get a full view of our new town in daylight. We were speechless. Not in our wildest dreams could we have envisioned anything like the vista which lay before us; a helter-skelter conglomeration of pathetic and squalid huts and shacks. Yet, we were saved the total carnage as all trash and garbage was still hidden beneath the snow.

Back in the mid-1860s some people lamented that the completion of the intercontinental railroad in the U.S. would be the end of the Old Raw West. They need not have worried. The Old Raw West was still very much alive and raw some 85 years later in the Yukon Territory. As a matter of fact, in some areas the lifestyle had regressed. Back in the 1800's the drinking water was purified by adding whisky, now chlorine was used for that purpose – hardly an improvement.

Many a romantic thought has been ascribed to life in the Yukon.

Steeped in eternal beauty - If you can see it through the clouds of mosquitoes.
Land for adventurous youth - Misguided and misinformed youth.
Once there, no one wants to leave - They can't scrape up enough money for the ticket to get out.
Abundance of open space in the Yukon - But what can you do with it?

Here are the facts. There are two seasons, one with subzero temperatures, the other with enough mosquitoes to choke a hippopotamus. As a matter of fact, during the short summer months a DC-3 would fly back and forth over the town at a few hundred feet, depositing heavy clouds of DDT in the futile effort to control the mosquito population. And let's not forget the black flies. The Indians called them "No see, no catch". There were plenty of those as well.

WORK

My toolmaker training was obviously of no use here – the industrial revolution had not yet reached this part of the globe. We all started working in my uncle's laundry. The obvious question was how could this kind of business possibly thrive in such an environment? As it turned out, it was better than a gold mine. My uncle had contracts with the Air Force, the Army and the hospital. They would bring their dirty wash to the laundry by the truck loads.

Because he was his very own brother, my uncle told my dad that he would start him off right at the very top rate of $1.10 an hour, which we later found out to be the going rate for unskilled labor and he didn't get a single raise over the next three years. My pay was $0.80 per hour and my mother's somewhat less.

My dad was the "chief laundry administrator"; he loaded and unloaded the washing machines, working like a madman from morning to night. My mother was "ironing assistant", she was one of several ladies ironing with a plain old iron on an ironing board. I was "boiler engineer". This meant bringing in wood for the ancient boiler and satisfying its voracious appetite for four foot long logs. In addition, I fixed leaky and frozen pipes. I also delivered laundry around town in a 1935 van. At that time, motor vehicles came equipped with a hand crank connected to the crank shaft to facilitate starting the engine if the starter didn't work, which in this case it never did. This abominable operation was bad enough in any conditions, but with the temperature well below zero, it became a nightmare.

Nothing more was ever mentioned about any business partnership. The laundry in Dawson City was pure fantasy; Dawson City was a ghost town. It became painfully clear that my uncle's objective to get us to leave Denmark was simply to get cheap, reliable labor – which he did.

A NEW WAY OF LIFE

In preparation for our arrival my dad rented a cabin which he thought to be affordable. A one room cabin. Wait, I am exaggerating. I must stick to the facts; "shack" would be a more fitting description.

To make it more attractive a few square feet had been walled off to create a "bedroom" big enough to accommodate one cot. Two cots could be squeezed into the so called "living room" which had a small table, three chairs and a couch. I have no idea why there were three chairs – there wasn't enough room for three people.

Another partition had been erected to create the illusion of a kitchen, with enough room for a wood burning stove and a water barrel, but no place to sit.

There was no running water which was just as well since the kitchen sink drained into a bucket which had to be emptied outside which you were reminded to do each time it overflowed. I quickly solved this problem by scrounging a piece of pipe, cut a hole in the wall, connected the pipe to the sink and poked the other end of the pipe out through the hole in the wall. Now we didn't have to go outside to dump the pail – pure luxury.

Water was purchased at 5 cent per bucket. This was not a problem as water was not consumed in vast quantities anyway. First off, it was not drinkable; the chlorine level was sufficient to water your eyes from across the room. This was probably a good thing as the water was pumped from the river at a hydro station located on the river bank downstream of a number of outhouses sitting on stilts in the water. Finding something suitable to drink was a problem. Milk was not to be had and the powdered version was absolutely disgusting. The only way to make the water drinkable was to add a lot of coffee, but even then the taste of the chlorine came through sharp and clear no matter how strong the coffee. Since beer at a dollar a bottle was out of reach as a substitute for water, chlorinated coffee became our main source of liquid intake.

No significant amount of water was used for bathing either as the only means of taking a bath in the cabin was to stand in a wash basin in the middle of the floor. But we were spared that ordeal while working for my uncle as we took our weekly bath by crawling into one of the washing machines at the laundry.

The general construction of the cabin made you wonder if it had been shipped there from the state of Kentucky. It looked like it was not intended to provide for human survival at temperatures much below 60°F, nevermind 60° below zero. The structure was elevated by stilts, leaving the floor exposed to the elements. Any liquid, other than rum, spilled on the floor of the cabin during the winter froze instantaneously and had to wait till spring to be cleaned. If there was any insulation in the walls or beneath the floor boards, it was not noticeable.

The place was equipped with a wood burning stove, apparently for the purpose of preventing frost bite. This was only partially successful. The problem was that once you got it fired up to maximum output, the side of your body facing the stove would be burned while the other side was freezing to death. Heating the stove to maximum temperature before going to bed did not prevent our blankets from being frozen to our lips by morning.

Wood was purchased by the cord. It was delivered in logs four feet long which then had to be sawed by hand into one foot long pieces to fit in the stove. I think we derived as much warmth from that operation as we did from burning the wood itself. We used about a cord of wood a week; at $18 per cord this placed a significant strain on our budget throughout the winter months.

In all fairness I should point out that the cabin was not totally void of amenities; it did have an outhouse. This worked well enough in the summer as it could be, and indeed was, emptied on a regular basis (another significant drain on the budget). However, it was problematic in the winter; how do you empty such a thing when the temperature continues to hover between 20 and 60° below zero? Well, you don't. The problem becomes obvious as the weeks go by, and eventually the solution is simple: when nature calls, you bring an ax – constipation was a godsend.

I have no idea as to how much we paid for rent, but at any rate it would have been too much.

So there we were, with all our oil paintings, Royal Copenhagen figurines, Bing and Grøndal china place setting for 12, with "Three Tower" genuine silverware, and crystal wine and liqueur glasses to match. Being keenly perceptive, it did not take long to recognize that it would be some time before any of this would be used again, and it all went into storage.

To this day I thoroughly regret not having taken a picture of that shack. Of course, at the time we were not particularly proud of living there, and when it came to photography I had not yet come to realize that some of the most treasured pictures are not necessary those of the good times.

GETTING ADJUSTED

We were exposed to a few more shocking events. The first came when I had to have a tooth pulled – I had to pay for it! No national health insurance. The fee was $10.00, which represented 12.5 hours of work – a financial blow.

As I thought about all this years later, I came to appreciate the enormous emotional impact this move must have had on my parents. They spend half their lives in a civilization where running water and central heating was taken for granted; a society where you can drive for hours and never see a house or farm in need of maintenance, nor a piece of discarded paper or garbage anywhere. They were accustomed to attending the best plays and musicals and frequented the best restaurants that Copenhagen, the Paris of Scandinavia, had to offer. Yet here they were, facing the challenge of readjusting to an entirely foreign environment and culture, not to mention the language problem. They tried to assimilate, but the gap was too great and the longing for the old days in Denmark never waned. Fortunately my mother had an indestructible sense of humor which helped immensely, but a few tears were shed late at night when no one appeared to notice.

I did not have much trouble with the language. About three months after arrival I was mistaken for being British because of the Oxford English accent left from my English lessons in grade school. My parent's struggle with English was a different matter. They were speaking Danish at home and at work which was catastrophic. Whether they liked it or not, they had to learn English or they would be trapped, with no possibility to move up. I soon realized that something had to be done. The only way I could help was to speak English only to them. I started doing this about four months after arriving in Whitehorse, and it was about the hardest thing I have ever done; speaking a foreign language to my own parents – nearly impossible, but I stuck with it. From then on, the only Danish I spoke to my parents were some occasional odd words just for fun.

As a 19 year old I did not have too many problems adjusting as I looked upon the whole situation as an adventure. But I must admit I missed my gliding and my friends back in Denmark, and found myself nostalgic for red tiled roofs.

MIRACLE

At one of my uncles' parties I mentioned that my life's dream was to become a pilot. My uncle leaped to his feet and pumped himself up: "You want to be a pilot?? No problem, I'll take care of that. Where is the phone book? Somebody hand me the phone book!" He thumbed through the phone book and with grand gestures he dialed the number, "Is this Whitehorse Flying School? This is Kai Gertsen (I was named after him) I got a nephew here that wants flying lessons. Yes! He can start tomorrow? OK." and hung up. He turned to me: "Don't you worry, everything is taken care of; you start flying lessons tomorrow."

I couldn't believe my ears. I had to take back everything I had said and thought about my uncle, and had been too hasty in my judgment. Perhaps I could become a bush pilot. This turn of events truly seemed like a miracle. Of course, when scrutinized, miracles invariably turn out to be illusions, but I was far too excited to ponder such axioms. I was in seventh heaven and pursued my flying lessons with vigor.

Naturally, this being the Yukon Territory, my instructor was a genuine bush pilot and, consequently, the training syllabus included exercises not usually practiced at other flying schools. Off-airport landings on frozen lakes were a favorite, which, by the way, were done without skis. Then before taking-off we would walk out on the ice, evaluate the snow conditions and select the optimum path for take-off – I had the time of my life.

My time in seventh heaven ran out sooner than I expected. When I received my next paycheck it was in the form of an "I owe you" which showed the sum my uncle had paid for my lessons less my wages. That entire performance at the party, "Your uncle will take care of this, don't you worry!" was put on entirely for show. Now I had just become an indebted laborer.

Still, I desperately wanted to continue pursuing my dream. After getting out of debt, I struggled on for a while, soloing after 9 hours followed by five more. But there comes a time when you no longer can stare reality in the face and deny it; working for $0.80 per hour and paying $16.00 per hour for flying time was not a viable combination – if only I could have given up the habit of eating.

DRIVERS LICENSE

Occasionally my uncle would let me drive his car. There were no paved streets and the roads were either muddy, slushy, or snow covered. Once I got stuck in the mud. Luckily, a sheriff stopped by and helped me out which was all very nice, but it did make me a little nervous. Surely, he would ask for the driver license I didn't have – I got lucky, he didn't ask.

When I relayed this incident to my uncle, he thought it might be a good idea for me to get a license.

Duly, I went to the motor vehicle bureau and told the clerk behind the counter, "I need a driver license." He looked at me, "Blue eyes, red hair, about 5 feet ten inches tall, and how much do you weigh?" "One hundred seventy pounds" I responded. "OK" he said "That will be two bucks." I paid the fee, he handed me the license – he never asked if I could drive a car!

FUN AND RECREATION

Now that flying was out of my reach, I had to find some other means of escaping the drudgery of work and have a bit of fun. But what in the world did people around here do for recreation? I knew that some people from the east of Canada actually came here to vacation. Surely it couldn't be just for a ride on a paddle wheel riverboat. Maybe the attraction was the vast wilderness and pure nature, and having been raised in civilized and urban surroundings, perhaps exploring nature would be fun.

I envisioned a tranquil, clear lake in an idyllic setting deep in the woods. Imagine taking a dip in a surrounding like that. In Denmark I swam in lakes, sometimes the ocean, and in the winter we would go to an indoor swimming pool in Copenhagen once a week, but this would be totally different; far removed from civilization, nothing but natural beauty all around – I could hardly wait.

When my uncle heard I was keen on swimming he thought he would offer us a real treat and drove us to a small lake for a picnic so I could go swimming. In this particular instance, I actually think his intensions were good.

We got to the lake, and it looked beautiful. As I undressed in the car, I could not fail but notice that I was being observed by about a million mosquitoes getting themselves all worked into a frenzy at the idea of what was about to happen. So as not to be totally devoured, I flung open the door of the car, sprinted down to the water, and dove in.

Having been raised near the North Atlantic I was accustomed to cold water, but this was unreal. I was amazed at the absence of ice. Nonetheless, I was not about to turn back and offer myself up to the mass of mosquitoes I had in hot pursuit so I plowed on toward a small island close to shore. I got there in record time, climbed out and made a revolting observation; I was covered with one inch long, black slimy blood suckers. I tried to brush them off, but they had just latched onto a great meal and were not about to give up that easy; they had to be pulled off one by one. This, of course, gave the mosquitoes an opportunity to close in. I looked for a spot in the water void of blood suckers - which turned out to be a waste of time. I had no choice but to dive back in. Back at the shore, the mosquitoes I had evaded earlier were eagerly awaiting my return. I sprinted to the car where I eventually recovered from the ordeal.

However, the fun wasn't over yet. Someone in our party got some kind of injury, so my uncle drove the injured to the hospital, leaving my dad and me to walk home. It was a several hour long walk, which we survived by using twigs to hit ourselves in the face or wherever else we got bitten in an attempt to keep the mosquitoes at bay, all the way home.

I must admit, the trip was a disappointment. I had more fun during a day at work – guess I was not the nature-boy I thought I was.

FACING REALITY

We eventually came to grips with the fact that the shack was too small for three people. One of us had to move out, and I was the obvious choice.

Then by a stroke of luck a job became available at the "grand" Whitehorse Inn which included room and board. This establishment is not to be confused with the Whitehorse Inn in the 1930 German operetta by the same name. In the musical, the charming Inn is located in the alpine idyll of upper Austria. There was nothing charming about The Whitehorse Inn of the Yukon. It was a big rectangular box, build strictly for practicality with no regard for aesthetics. Yet, it was the grandest building in town.

The job opening was for a boiler engineer, and I just happened to be one so I applied and got the job. I must say the term engineer was a misnomer. The job simply consisted of feeding the boiler with four foot long logs.

Leaving the job at the laundry was not difficult as my reverence for my uncle had dropped a peck or two since the days I listened to the stories about him at my grandparents' dining room table.

During the summer months when the Inn's boiler didn't need stoking, I performed other miscellaneous tasks such as cutting ice on the river for the ice house. The Inn had no refrigerators, and I don't think anyone else did either, at least I never saw one. The ice house was a small, well insulated building and the ice was buried in saw dust. This actually worked quite well with the ice lasting throughout the entire year.

The owner of the Inn was a big, robust character. He and his wife had regular high volume tiffs, for which I had a front row seat in that the boiler room was directly below their window. So how did he get to be the richest man in town? Very simple; he won the Whitehorse Inn in a poker game. He used to own a butcher shop which he bet against the Inn, and that just happened to be his lucky day. He had two sons who constantly drove around town stone drunk. Every time they crashed a car it was because of a tooth ache, migraine headache, etc., but in keeping with the customs of the old, raw West, being the richest man in town had it advantages, and his boys were never arrested.

Obviously, swimming in mountain lakes was not the way to enjoy the wilderness of the Yukon. So with everyone talking about fishing, obviously, that must be *the* big attraction. The only problem was that I had no interest in fishing, in fact, I positively disliked it. Just the same, I had to have some recreation whether I liked it or not.

On a bright midsummer's morning I climbed into an open truck with a group of bushwhackers to join them on one of their routine overnight fishing trips into the Canadian tundra. About 35 miles out along the Alaskan highway the truck was parked and we started our hike through the bush toward the fishing spot following our leader, a rugged, grubby old timer who we had a tough time keeping up with.

We were surrounded by mosquitoes the instant we stopped the truck, and two steps into the woods we were covered with them – I was overpowered. The old timer pulled a bottle of repellent out of his pocket, "here, put some of this stuff on!" By the time I had rubbed some of that in my hands in preparation to cover my face it was a gel composed 50% of mosquitoes. "How in the world do you cope with this?" I asked. "Ah, just ignore it" was his response. The hike through the woods turned out to be a real treat.

As we arrived at our destination, someone had the idea that maybe the fishing would be better on the island a short distance from shore. This apparently was the first time anyone had suggested this and there was no means of getting there. So we built a raft. Trees were cut down, trimmed and lashed together. Testing was done by the old timer. On the first launch the raft followed the bottom of the lake as he pushed off – a sure sign that a couple more logs were needed to keep it afloat.

When it became time for dinner, I volunteered to do the cooking. "Where are the cooking utensils," I asked. Our leader pointed up at a tree "that is where we store them." Sure enough, there they were, pans, pots, and all. I pulled down a frying pan. In my entire life, I had never seen anything more disgusting; it was covered with a thick coating of grease loaded with spiders and bugs. I showed him the pan, holding it far away from me, "what do I do with this?" I asked. "No problem," he said, pulled off his hat, made a couple of wiping circles in the pan, straightened out his hat and put it back on as he handed me the pan – I almost passes out.

I had brought our dog, which I think was a cross between a German shepherd and a wolf. Not a seasoned woodsman, I was ill prepared to spend the night outside in the wilderness and all I had brought was a thin blanket. Even in midsummer the temperature here dropped close to freezing at night, but that does have one significant advantage in that the mosquitoes can't get off the ground. Nonetheless, the cold was a problem, and the dog and I spend the first couple of hours pushing each other from under the blanket till she finally gave up and went home, and arrived there two weeks later – it was a long night.

So was fishing more fun than working? – I wasn't convinced.

JOB APPLICATION

When applying for a job all you had to do was convince your prospective employer you could do the job. This was quite different from the country I came from where to secure any kind of employment you needed to have a degree, completed an apprenticeship or other official training program, and submit all documentation along with the necessary affidavits. Here, if someone needed a plumber, you simply said you could do the job and chances were they would try you out. This system worked well for me. During my three years in Whitehorse I was a sign painter, plumber, truck driver, and boiler engineer for the Air Force, which was slightly more technical than the job at the laundry or the Whitehorse Inn, as they operated several boilers fueled by oil.

I was only turned down for one job; that of a heavy-duty truck driver. I had never driven a heavy truck before and the fellow that checked me out did not like the way I handled the double-clutch-downshift. All the idiot should have done was to give me half an hour to figure it out and I most likely would have gotten the job.

When I took the job as plumber for the Air Force, I figured it a fairly safe bet in that plumbing required some of the same skills as those of a toolmaker, like envisioning how things go together and having a certain mechanical aptitude.

They put me to the test right away. An officer's barrack had just been erected and my instructions were to go and install the plumbing which included hooking up the toilet to the septic tank. At that time sewer pipes were connected with a flange stuffed with hemp and sealed with lead. They told me where the toilet and bathroom were to be and left me to it. I finished the job unaided and didn't have a single complaint.

BUILDING OUR HOUSE

It soon became clear that if we were to make any headway in this place, we had to build a house.

We found a plot of land. This wasn't purchased, but rented from the government for a period of 99 years at the exorbitant fee of $1. The construction got off to a good start when my benevolent uncle, through his contacts, managed to purchase half of an army barrack for us at the special deal of $150. Only much later did we find out he had paid $100. Nonetheless, half a barrack was better than starting from scratch.

With much enthusiasm we got started. The good news was that between our efforts to make money and working on the house there was absolutely no time to chase after any further recreational pursuits – what a relief.

We decided to spare nothing; our new house was to have all the comforts civilization had to offer. It was to have a basement, central heating, and indoor bathroom - the works.

For a while we struggled with the decision to either dig the basement by hand or go for the extravagance of hiring someone to bulldoze it – we went with the bulldozer. The excavation for the basement was only four feet deep. Posts to support the retaining walls needed to prevent the dirt from caving in were positioned at 7 foot spacing around the perimeter.

Then we dug a well. We got all excited when we reached water – we had struck it rich; the water was thick with oil. Our excitement quickly abated when we discovered that our plot of land had been a landfill for the Air Force during the war. Our only gain was a can of peaches that we dug up. The water was obviously going to have some restrictions in usage.

Then we suffered a major set-back. One day, driving to our new estate, we noticed flood waters that got higher as we got closer. The scene that greeted us upon arrival was disheartening. Water was flowing in at one end of the structure and out the other. Half of the posts intended as support for the cellar walls were floating, as was the supporting structure of our well. The reason for this calamity was that our plot was just beneath the 700 foot high plateau (known as *the mountain*) where the Army and Air Force bases were located, and a main water line had broken. There we were, back to start. The good news was that the barrack had not yet been moved into place.

For a long time life was nothing but work on the job, and work on the house. Of course, we moved in long before it was finished. Actually, I don't think we *ever* finished it. In the new house there was room for all of us so I quit the job at the Whitehorse Inn. And since I was no longer able to use the convenience of the washing machines at my uncle's laundry, a bath now meant standing in a wash basin in the middle of the floor. Occasionally I would splurge and go to the barber and spend $0.75 for a shower.

The septic tank and plumbing was still in the planning stage when we moved in, but we insisted on having the toilet inside. With plenty of chemicals this worked well enough, and having some land around the house allowed us to simply dig a hole when it was time to empty the pot. Fortunately, we went through this phase in the septic construction during the summer. It was important to keep close track of exactly where we buried the treasures, as it was best to avoid digging in the same spot twice. Good thing was that we need not worry about digging holes in the lawn as there wasn't any – there was no grass anywhere. I suppose the combination of barren dirt and the short growing season kept grass and weeds at bay. I believe the only way to acquire a lawn was to purchase one from Edmonton. Once I actually heard a rumor of someone having a lawn, but I never got to see it.

We were forced to compromise on some of our planned amenities. The basement was somewhat below standard in that it had a dirt floor and part of the walls were dirt as well, and you couldn't stand up straight. But we did have central heating. The furnace, installation and all, was home built. It was a forced air system driven by convection. It really worked rather well; a couple of hefty logs at bedtime kept the place from getting excessively cold, although it did not prevent rime ice from forming on the inside nail heads.

I must have become restless and felt a need for a change or a bit of adventure, because I signed up as cabin boy on one of the river boats. My dad almost exploded. "What is going to happen to the house?? I need you on the house." Didn't have much choice, went back, apologized and told them I was not able to take the job due to circumstances beyond my control.

When it got to be time to install the plumbing I was up to the task after my experience as plumber for the Air Force. I must admit, the septic tank being constructed of regular two by sixes would not have met code if there had been one, but we figured it would last as long as we needed it. Our plans were to get out of the Yukon as soon as we had enough money for a ticket.

Somewhere along the way we had a bit of luck. A friend of mine by the name of Mike bought a truck which allowed the two of us to go into the woods and cut all the firewood needed for the winter – a true wind fall. The next step was to construct an enclosed porch to store the wood, this way we could cut all winter's fire wood and store it inside – pure luxury.

The challenge of providing hot running water was met rather ingeniously, I thought, by running pipes through the furnace in a serpentine pattern. This did have one drawback in that there would not be hot water in the summer time, but what the heck – summers were short.

There were other compromises, like skipping a foundation. It turned out to be a bit of an adventure living in a house without a foundation. You never knew when entering the living room if you would walk uphill or downhill and from time to time it became necessary to level the floor. This was accomplished by going down below, jack up a little here and down a little there to reduce the angle of the slope.

We got along quite well without an architect; we didn't even make a sketch. We just paced off the rooms, erected the partitions, and had no regrets.

In spite of all these shortcuts and savings we must have invested a small fortune in the place. Probably somewhere near $1,000 but a good deal of that was spent on furniture. We didn't think of keeping track. Nothing was bought on credit. One month we might have enough money for a window, next month for some wall paper and plumbing hardware, and so on. When my parents left the Yukon they sold it for $3,000. The hefty profit was used to finance their move to Hamilton.

Our new house was a huge improvement from the shack, but we remained deprived of the esteem derived from living on a street with a name. Then again, I should point out that it was really only a path.

NOTEWORTHY

In spite of us being on the very lowest rung on the social ladder, my parents were readily accepted by the Whitehorse community. They had always had the uncanny ability to blend in with people from all walks of life. Initially, living in the shack did limit their integration in this regard, but once we moved into our *new house* it didn't take long for things to change.

In short order they joined a bridge club. This was while my mother had the distinguished job of being a dishwasher for the Air Force. That did not bother the doctor or the attorney who were part of the bridge club.

For those who are not familiar with the game of bridge, it is a game that tends to be taken somewhat seriously by those who pursue it. The bidding of the hands at play is typically guided by a well-defined point system. Since my parents didn't know anything about that system, their bidding was totally unconventional. Such deviation from convention would be intolerable to most bridge players, but not in this case. They all took it in stride and my parent's virtual non existing knowledge of the English language didn't seem to matter either. I do think my dad redeemed himself in their eyes by his uncanny ability to remember all the cards played so when the game got down to the end play, he had it all figured out and knew who held which remaining cards.

What we referred to as our house really more closely resembled a big cabin, and there is no denying it; we lived in a shanty town. But the interior was a different story. All rooms were wallpapered, and my parents had spared no

71

money on furniture, as it was all quality stuff. The grand oil paintings, crystal stemware, Royal Copenhagen porcelain figurines, and the twelve piece Bing and Grøndal china and silverware, had all been brought out of storage.

Visitors were treated to an amazing transformation upon entering this forlorn abode located in the midst of a squalid cabin neighborhood. Leaving the outside world behind, they walked into a setting reminiscent of a cozy, Danish country home.

60° F BELOW ZERO

Mark Twain once wrote: "It was so cold the mercury was at the bottom of the tube. If the thermometer had been any longer we would all have frozen to death."

It was New Year's Eve and we were going to a ball at the Whitehorse Inn. My parents still enjoyed a good time and this was the one time a year they splurged. It was brutally cold, and we lived a couple of miles from town and needed a taxi. Yes, in spite of the primitive conditions there were still such things as taxis. The problem however was that we didn't have a phone, so I was elected to walk into town to fetch a taxi.

Dressed in a two piece suit, a dressy top coat and dress shoes, it didn't take long before I fully respected the northern winter climate. Soon the skin on my legs felt as if it was frozen solid, and before long the prospect of reaching my destination was getting doubtful. It still surprises me that I actually made it. Yes, the official temperature was 60° F below zero, the lowest temperature in Whitehorse while we lived there, and I was fortunate not to miss the event. During our first winter we were told we should have been there the previous winter when the temperature dropped to 84° F below zero. The pipes above the boiler at the Air Force base had frozen. Well, one's timing can't always be right. It should be noted that all this was before the wind chill factor was invented.

Another interesting aspect of the local culture was that when it came to dancing at the Whitehorse Inn, just about everybody got dressed fit for the Waldorf Astoria. Of course there were always two or three miners who apparently had just gotten off their dog sled, returning from their gold mine. They would stomp around the dance floor in the only set of clothes they owned, having a great time.

One local custom that was hard for us to comprehend were the draconian laws regarding the consumption of alcohol. At the Whitehorse Inn every guest would bring a paper bag containing a bottle of whisky which was immediately placed under the table. This, to us, was an odd thing to do since everyone, including the chief of police, knew what was in it. The next step was to order a "set up." This consisted of Ginger Ale and ice cubes and everyone knew what that was for as well. When pouring the whisky, care had to be taken that the content of the bag remained hidden. Then came the real zinger; since it was illegal to drive with an open bottle in the car, all bottles had to be consumed before leaving with the result that most of the folks got to be falling-down drunk.

There was no other place in town where you could enjoy a cocktail or have a meal with a glass of wine. To my recollection, the only restaurant was at the Whitehorse Inn, and they did not serve alcoholic beverages.

Then there were the Beer Parlors – men only establishments. Must be we didn't try hard enough, but we never managed to see the rhyme or reason to go there.

ANOTHER JOB FROM HELL

When I was shoveling saw dust in Denmark from morning till night I thought it was the worse job in the world; little did I know.

This lady had a water delivery business consisting of a door-less, ancient truck with a water tank. The one thing that appealed to me about this job was that the pay was a fixed weekly amount. Inasmuch as I considered myself to be someone who could work considerably harder than the average of my peers, I figured I should be able to make this deal work out at something well above a dollar an hour. So I took the job.

The1939 movie "Gunga Din," based loosely on the poem by Rudyard Kipling, takes place in India. "Gunga Din" is the Indian word for water bearer. In the movie a Gunga Din who carried water for the soldiers, had as his greatest aspiration to become a soldier himself. Here I was, just another Gunga Din, but one who wanted to become a pilot. The notable difference being that I was a water delivery boy in the midst of the Yukon winter. The thing we had in common was that our respective goals in life were beyond our reach.

The job required picking up the truck in the morning, driving it to the power station to fill up the tank, and then deliver water by the bucket to 158 customers. That's right, bucket. This was not a high tech operation, no pump, no hose. I ran back and forth with those buckets all day, every day. When I came home, totally exhausted, I barely managed to struggle out of my frozen pants and stand them up in the corner where they remained standing for quite some time.

The truck was not so easy to wake up in the morning when the thermometer was hovering around 40° F below. I often had to resort to heating the engine block with a blow torch. There were times I even thought of lighting a bonfire beneath the block.

The deliveries to the shops along Main Street were made from the back ally where I made an interesting discovery. Those grand buildings on Main Street were nothing but simple cabins with a facade on the front.

No matter how hard I worked, I could not get my hourly rate above $0.65 an hour.

Then followed a couple of weeks where I didn't get paid. When it became obvious no pay was forthcoming, I quit and took her to small claims court. After the judge ruled in my favor he told my former employer that not only had she caused me trouble by holding back my pay, but she had caused me to lose my job, to which she replied: "Oh, he can come back and work for me anytime." The humor in that statement didn't escape many in the court room.

INDIANS

The water delivery job did provide me with a bit of adventure. As it were, I had a few Yukon Indians on my customer list. Consequently, I was allowed the privilege to visit various Indian homes throughout the week. I have no idea what they used the water for, as the water was undrinkable and they most certainly didn't use it for washing.

During my first water delivery to an Indian abode I went into shock, my windpipes closed and I couldn't breathe. The smell would have been enough to drop the proverbial vulture off the manure wagon. Right there and then I learned to hold my breath while delivering water and collecting the nickel – thinking of it now, I probably didn't smell much better myself.

The typical abode was roughly 10 by 15 feet or smaller, with the lower few feet of the walls constructed of discarded corrugated sheet metal and bits of old wooden boards, and the upper part consisting of pieces of tarp held in place by some rickety support structure. The furniture consisted of shipping crates and boxes, placed along the walls. In one corner there was a child of about two or three years old anchored to an old mattress. The center piece was a wood burning stove.

My image of Indians was derived from Hollywood movies: strong, wise, and proud. The Indians of the Yukon were a disappointment to me as they seemed to be content with a very empty and docile existence.

Upon entering their shelter I would typically find three or four Indians sitting on crates, facing each other with their eyes and mind not focused on anything in particular.

During extended observations, none of them seemed to make a move until the fire in the stove was almost out. Then one of them would go outside and cut one piece of wood, but never two. Apparently they didn't have much faith in the future. It was as if they had no concept of "future". On rare occasions one would take on a job. If at the end of the day he got paid for the day's work, he would quit. He would then have enough money for a bottle of whisky and a can of sardines, and there was no need for anything more. A different approach to life – and who is to say who is right.

SAILING

Now that work on the house had eased up, my thoughts once again turned to recreational activity.

The dream of gliding never vanished, and from time to time I would contemplate the possibility of building a Grunau Baby. But time and again I was forced to admit that such project was positively, totally hopelessly impossible.

Sailing however was a possibility. It would definitely be a lot easier to build a boat than a glider. I had always been attracted to the sea and surely, had I not discovered gliding I would have pursued sailing with the same vigor. When I suggested to my friend Mike that we should build a sailboat, he was all for it.

This was not exactly state-of-the-art boat building. The framework was constructed of some trim-wood left over from the barrack, so there was no need for drawings since the size of the boat was determined by the length of the trim strips. We scrounged some kind of fabric to cover the hull, which we waterproofed with left-over paint. I am reasonably sure an old bed sheet served as the sail. Considering everything, we thought it was a pretty neat boat, and the price was right.

When the great day of her maiden voyage arrived, our proud creation was loaded onto Mike's truck and we headed for the lake. The conditions were perfect; a nice off-shore breeze, we couldn't have asked for anything better. The sail was hoisted - we shoved off. What a success; we skimmed over the water in fine style, probably the only sailboat ever to have plied the waves of a Yukon lake. In short order we had covered quite some distance so we thought it might be prudent to see how well she would tack. This turned out to be a disappointment when the rudder broke off. Now there was only one thing to do, sit back and enjoy the trip to the downwind shore of the lake. Fortunately it wasn't too big a lake, but sadly it was far too long a hike back to the truck to carry the boat, so we had no choice but to leave our pride and joy behind.

In my dreams, I envision some day in the distant future when a group of anthropologists stumble upon the remains of our boat. It won't take them long to recognize the Viking origin of the design and rightfully deduce that the Vikings did indeed make it all the way north to the Yukon.

HEADING EAST

In early 1951, we were visited by another uncle; this was the good one, the uncle from the *east*. This was my mother's brother who was living in Toronto at the time. He encouraged me to join him and was certain I could find a job in my trade in Toronto, despite the fact that I hadn't actually completed my apprenticeship.

So, on a nice spring day in 1951 it was the old story all over again. Getting on an airplane, flying off to a different culture and new life with little more than the clothes I was wearing and $25 in my pocket. Only this time, I was the one to venture out first to reconnoiter the lay of the land. And this time the opportunities were significantly more promising. Yet, it took two more years to get back into gliding.

NO REGRETS

All in all, I really have no regrets regarding the time we lived in the Yukon. It was one hell of an adventure. I didn't realize it then, but the downside was that it had left me a few strides behind my future peers who at my age had already secured years of higher education – I had a lot of catching up to do. On the other hand, how many people in today's world can lay claim to such an immense array of life experiences which have given me many marvelous reference points for the rest of my life. To this very day, there are times when in the shower, I am overcome with gratitude when warm water cascades over my body after the simple act of turning on the faucet.

My first place of work, my uncle's laundry

Our new upgrade neighborhood in the foreground

Our dream house under construction

Our neighbor's – no wonder we were proud of ours

Pursuing my dream for a moment in time

Harvesting ice for the Whitehorse Inn

Hired on as a cabin boy

The grandest place in town – The Whitehorse Inn

My friend Mike inspecting our progress

The pride of the neighborhood – finished at last

Chapter 4

RETURN TO CIVILIZATION

So, there I was, getting off a DC-3 at the Toronto airport after three years in the Yukon Territory, with little more to my name or in my pockets than when I arrived there. There were two significant differences however; I was back in civilization and greeted by a much more reasonable member of the family, my mother's brother who had emigrated to the United States when he was young. This uncle, Bill Clausen, was on temporary assignment in Canada for the company he worked for in the United States. His outstanding character trait was a delightful sense of humor which he shared with my mother.

Hoping to find a job in my intended trade, I spent the first week beating the bushes in Toronto, but no luck. My three years in the Yukon probably didn't help. Then a little push from my uncle did the trick. My uncle knew someone at Westinghouse in Hamilton. It is absolutely amazing what a word or two in the right place can accomplish; I was hired as a tool maker in spite of not having completed my apprenticeship.

My starting wage was $1.57 per hour – from rags to riches overnight. Not only did that represent a 50% increase in wages from the Yukon, but the stores were loaded with wares at half the price of what I had become accustomed to. The reduced cost of shipping things to Toronto as opposed to the Yukon made a world of difference.

I was fortunate to find a room to rent within walking distance of my place of work. In short order I settled into a routine. I lived frugal. Dinners consisted of open faced, banana and raisin sandwiches. It would be a year before I got a car, and in the meanwhile my savings account grew. When summer came there were many bus trips to the Sunnyside Pool in Toronto.

Not much progress was made about getting back into gliding. There had to be gliding going on somewhere, but I had no idea how to find it. As the sport of gliding remains to this day, it was a well-kept secret.

A MOST SIGNIFICANT EVENT

In short order I succeeded in making contact with other Danes and joined the Danish Club of Hamilton. During the winter months they put on a dance at the Windsor Hotel.

In another part of Hamilton, there was a girl by the name of Helga Kjær Pedersen, yes, of Danish descent, sharing a room with a girlfriend by the name of Simone. Simone had been attending some of those dance affairs and had tried, unsuccessfully, to get Helga to come along. Well, Helga had once attended a similar Swedish party and had not been favorably impressed. Simone tried to convince her friend that there was a difference between Swedes and Danes, but Helga was not easily convinced. Simone pleaded once more, "This will be the last dance of the season." Was it luck or fate? Helga caved in, and that decision was the turning point in my life.

The minute I spotted her I simply knew she was the one and only, but the competition was stiff. There was another fellow on the same pursuit and every time the music started we almost fell over each other to get to this girl first. I still remember her dress, her smile, and my vision for the future.

MANIC DEPRESSION

For some reason I had the impression Helga felt the same way about me as I did for her, but then doubts started to creep in. When trying to set up a date there were headaches, other engagements, working late, not feeling good, etc., etc., etc. Desperate for some good advice, I confided in my friend, "What am I going to do?" "Ha" he answered "when you miss one bus there will always be another coming along." Well, that was not much help, as this was the bus I wanted.

A MOST DELIGHTFUL TURN OF EVENTS

When I finally got the elusive date, what happens? After having had a leisurely drink at a bar we strolled outside and headed for the car. The only problem was I couldn't remember where I had parked it. Regardless, I nonchalantly walked on, bravely displaying all the confidence in the world as if I knew where I was going, desperately hoping the d . . . . car would show up. No such luck. Only after traversing several downtown streets was the lost vehicle recovered. This was surely no way to impress the girl of my dreams. I was certain this episode would doom all my hopes and aspirations. But Helga was more forgiving than I anticipated - as she has been ever since.

It wasn't long thereafter, when dancing under the stars to a live orchestra at an outdoors restaurant, that I asked her to marry me. I vividly remember her smile and the look in her eyes as she looked up at me and said yes.

REDISCOVERING GLIDING

Eventually I made contact with three fellows that owned a glider. It was Charlie Yeates, Norm Russ and Roy Burn. Charlie Yeates was the driving force.

Later, Charlie became one of the pillars in Canadian gliding and remains active to this day.

One evening, when I had a date with Helga, I got a phone call from Charlie; could I come up to Mt. Hope airport and help them rig a glider? That couldn't take more than half an hour, I thought. Helga could come with me and wait while we assembled the thing.

I went into a state of shock as we entered the hangar. There was this abomination known as a TG-3 stowed on an open trailer. There was no resemblance to the graceful and elegant gliders I had envisioned to find in Canada when I left Denmark, nor to any glider I'd ever seen for that matter. This huge monster was designed and built for military training, intended to be rigged once and never again. It gave the impression of weighing a thousand pounds, which it did. The four of us struggled for three hours to assemble it. That may well have been the first time in history a task of this magnitude had ever been accomplished by just four men. Meanwhile Helga sat in a corner of the cold hangar for the entire duration. Following such display of blatant disregard, you would think any reasonable girl would have terminated our relationship, but she didn't. Obviously, she was made of the right stuff. On April 24, 1953, we got married.

It seemed to me that the population of Hamilton ought to be able to sustain a gliding club so I set out to establish one. I succeeded in rounding up about ten enthusiasts. The next step was to get a glider. As money would likely be in short supply, I felt lucky to find a glider of some antiquity which needed some work. Before long, I grew a little concerned as to whether the troops I had rounded up would be up to the task of making this thing flyable. I need not have worried, when it came time to collect the initiation fees they all caved in, but there were still plenty of excuses; just bought a car, need to have the house painted, just bought new furniture, etc. etc.

INSTRUCTOR FOR THE AIR CADETS

That was when lady luck paid me another visit. Somehow I got word that The Royal Canadian Air Cadets were starting a glider training program. To this end, they had purchased a Schweizer 2-22, and needed an instructor. This was in June of 1953. My qualifications were somewhat shaky, and the record keeping of my flying in Denmark had not been up to Canadian standards.

During my gliding in Denmark we did not have individual pilot log books. Our flights were recorded and maintained by the club, and only the number of flights was kept track of - flight time was not logged. The reason for that might have been that the flights were measured in seconds, and no one had a stop watch. My records showed 150 flights, including one thermal flight of half an hour. Based on my best guesstimate of flight time it came to a grand total of 4 hours and 45 minutes, not bad for just 3½ years of total devotion to the work shop, but would that be good enough to get me the job? Fortunately I discovered a handy provision in the rules that let you log any flight that includes a 360 degree turn, at 6 minutes. This bit of recalculating brought my total flight time up to 47 hours and 45 minutes, very impressive indeed, and I got the job. I suspect I was the only applicant.

This situation turned out better than expected. The Air Cadets were not able to obtain insurance coverage which prevented the program from getting off the ground. The net result was that I had a Schweizer 2-22 all to myself, to fly whenever I felt like it. Following a check-out by Charlie Yeates, I got straight to work – flying as much as possible.

The only drawback was that the Air Cadets had neglected to purchase a trailer. Staying close to the home field would be crucial, especially in a 2-22. The basic design of this glider has much in common with gliders of the 1930's, and the performance is no exception.

Here comes the interesting part. Following the initial arrangements, I do not recall having any further contact with the powers that be at the Air Cadet program. The renumeration for my services however arrived anually by check in the mail in the amount of $85.00. Apparently, some bureaucrats are not too particular as to how they spend the taxpayers money, but I didn't complain. The checks stopped coming after we moved to the US. Now that I think about it, if I had left a forwarding address, those checks might still be arriving annually to this day.

HELGA'S AIR TRAVEL

A gliding camp was scheduled in August of 1953 at a small airstrip near Kitchener. This was no contest, but just a chance to get together with other like-minded folks for a week of flying and companionship. This could be worthwhile. The only problem was how to get the glider there since I had no trailer. That stumbling block was easily crossed when Norm Russ offered to tow the Schweizer 2-22 there with his Stinson. Our 1939 Pontiac was in the shop for a couple of days (not unusual), but Helga could ride with me in the glider while a friend had volunteered to drive the car there in a couple of days.

There we were, ready to go. Helga sitting in the back with a small suitcase on her lap, the only travel, as such, by glider that I know of. The cloud base was 500 feet. Just before we left, Norm came back and confided in me that I should be prepared, as he might have to cut me loose if conditions deteriorated any further. Helga immediately came to life: "What did he say, what did he say?" "Oh" I responded, "He just said the weather looks fine and it looks like we are going to have a nice trip." Which we did.

AN ALL TIME RECORD, OF SORTS

The next day shaped up to be a superb flying day. The perfect day for a five hour flight to qualify for my FAI silver "C" duration badge.

I was ready to go. Barograph installed and a thermo with liquid refreshment stowed away.

I was off right about 12 o'clock. After tow, I went straight to 3,000 feet under a blue sky. Some nice looking clouds were forming just a short distance from the field. My reasoning was this; as long as I will be staying up for 5 hours, it makes no difference whether I spend my time over there under the clouds or over the airport, so why not go where the clouds are marking the thermals?

Forty-seven minutes after takeoff I was sitting in a field 5 miles from the airport. Under normal circumstances this would not have been a problem. I would simply call my crew, who would have come to my rescue in short order with a trailer, promptly de-rigged the glider, and we would have been back home in no time, but this situation was far from normal.

My first request, as I called the airport from the farm house, was if it would be possible to stir up a crew. The fellow I talked to sounded very excited and helpful and was quite sure he could manage that. He would call me back when he got someone lined up.

A short while later my involuntarily crew chief was back on the phone "It was not much of a problem and they will be on their way shortly, just tell us where your rig is parked." I had to confess that there was a slight predicament, as I didn't have a trailer. The line went quiet, "what do you mean, you don't have a trailer?" Apparently I had ventured where no man had gone before. I tenderly probed as to the possibility that there might be a trailer somewhere in the back of the hangar that could conceivably fit a Schweizer 2-22. The owner of the voice at the other end of the line was not optimistic and seemed to be losing some of his enthusiasm for this retrieve. Nevertheless, he would see what he could do.

Before he could hang up, I dropped the other bomb. "I know this is somewhat awkward, but I don't have a car either." I thought I could actually sense the temperature drop a few degrees over the line. "What do you mean, you don't have a car?" He snapped back. So I explained the situation and he softened ever so slightly, "Well, we will see what we can do."

I wasn't feeling too comfortable about this state of affairs myself, but unfortunately I had no choice but to press on; could he bring some tools as well, as I didn't have any, and maybe find someone who knew how to de-rig this thing as I had never taken one apart before? No doubt, by this time, his thoughts of me were not of the complementary variety.

Sometime later in the afternoon my disenchanted rescuers appeared, with a trailer in tow no less.

As the day went on, the prospect of a successful retrieve began to evaporate. As Mark Twain put it, we had to "grab the bull by the tail, and face the situation," - we could not make the trailer fit. "Could there be another trailer in the back of the hangar?" I ventured. My crew was not optimistic and was plainly not happy. Nonetheless, they rose to the challenge.

Late evening they re-appeared, not only with another trailer, but a full set of tools and an expert in de-rigging a 2-22. Now things were looking up, and success might still be within our grasp. We finally succeeded in securing the glider to the trailer and were on our way home.

It was close to 10 pm as we rolled onto the airport – nine hours for a 5 mile retrieve. Considering that I had landed in a perfect field with easy access and nothing to hamper the retrieve such as having to be extracted from a swamp or trees, freed from the confines of a military compound, or being denied access to the glider by a disgruntled farmer, it surely had to be an all-time record.

Sometime later, contemplating this event, I came to realize the experience had not been all negative. Having covered some distance, although short, had left some sense of accomplishment. Imagine releasing from tow and purposefully heading out into the unknown? What a thrill that would be. The more I thought about it, flying distance on purpose surely seemed like something worthwhile pursuing. Of course, that dream had to wait till a glider with a trailer became accessible. Just the same, I promptly added a column in my sailplane log book labeled "Distance" and entered my first cross-country flight. Little did I know the day would come when every single one of my flights would be in pursuit of distance.

SILVER "C"

Before my job for the Canadian Air Cadets came to an end, I did succeed in getting my five hour duration required for the FAI silver "C" badge. That was May of 1954, nine years after qualifying for the Danish "C" certificate.

We had two weekend days with spectacular weather. The flight of the day before had been 4 hours and 18 minutes, and the day wasn't done yet, but there was no point staying up any longer as I did not have a barograph. The next day I borrowed one on which I recorded 6 hours and 23 minutes. In spite of a lack of bladder relief accommodations and being strapped to a seat consisting of two pieces of plywood mounted at a 90° angle to one another, I do not remember any discomfort. Today I wouldn't last an hour – ah, to be young again.

A LATER CANADIAN ADVENTURE

A few years later at Brantford, Canada, I had the privilege to experience a flight in a TG-3 being towed by a Tiger Moth, hardly a match for a thousand pound glider. The first challenge was to clear the 3 foot fence at the far end of the field, which was only made possible by some help from ground effect. Just as a crash into the fence seemed imminent, my mind was put at ease by a soft voice from the back seat assuring me the situation was normal. Then followed a jolly ride with a close look at the scenery while looking for bits of lift without which we were going nowhere – those Canadians know how to have fun. The average tow was 15 minutes. This really made it a bargain at the price of $2.50.

GLIDING ON HOLD ONCE AGAIN

At that time, a number of our friends moved to the United States. As far as we were concerned that was simply motivated by a "the grass is always greener on the other side" syndrome. Then one day there was a notice in the paper, "Ford Motor Company in Buffalo seeking toolmakers. Starting wage $3.00 an hour. Apply at the Canuck Hotel." It got my attention. I had been at the top of the wage scale for toolmakers in Canada for some time now, which was $2.10 an hour. Thirty percent increase – it was worth checking out. I took the job.

Returning to our humble abode at the end of the day, Helga had her back to me in the process of cooking some pork chops. "Guess what," I said "we are moving to the States. I have taken a job with the Ford Motor Company." She didn't even turn around, "That's fine" was her response. How many women are there like that? Maybe one in ten thousand. And so it came to pass that three months later we moved to Buffalo, NY. Being sponsored by the Ford Company significantly reduced the waiting time for entering The United States.

What I did not realize till later was that the demands of the job were incompatible with any kind of hobby – especially gliding. Another year of gliding was to be lost.

Hamilton, 1952

Our Wedding Day, April 24, 1953

Chapter 5[1]

LAND OF DREAMS

In the spring of 1955 we left Canada, filled with high hopes for a glorious future in the United States of America - the land of dreams. It did not take long before I realized that some of my dreams had to wait until after I got through the nightmares.

ARRIVAL

I don't recall what I expected of the job at Ford, but it certainly was not what it turned out to be. The first blow was the schedule; every other Sunday off. I had managed to locate a gliding operation near Batavia, about 40 miles away, but with only one day off every other week, it was pointless to even think about joining them. That one day off turned into a flurry of activity, trying to cram four days of R&R into one.

The job turned out to be a far cry from any I had embarked on previously. It was a stamping plant, producing car body panels, using heavy 500 ton presses several stories high with a noise level beyond any known scale. Add to that a grimly lit work environment, and it left a lot to be desired. Once a shift started the gates were locked and leaving early was not an option. Well, maybe in the event of death.

Much of the time we worked 10 hour days. This was the upside; I worked all hours every chance I had and made more money than I ever hoped for, but this sure had its consequences since being low in seniority meant that I was assigned the afternoon shift for months in a row. Our main recreation and relaxation was playing canasta with some friends from 2-5 in the morning. I hated the job but felt I had some obligation considering Ford Company had sponsored me for the necessary paperwork that allowed me to enter and work in the US. After one and a half years I felt I had served my time.

SETTLING IN

On one of those Sundays we drove to Rochester, NY. We took a liking to the

---

[1] This chapter was started by Kai, and finished by his daughters Linda and Cindy based on taped conversations with their father during the last weeks of his life.

city and decided to move there. This was the spring of 1957, and I found a job and a flat to rent. Having actively sought out the Rochester Soaring Club, I joined in no time.

This was when another turning point in my life occurred; I met the Seymour family. It was a perfect match from day one. Their two sons, David and John, were in their teens (12 and 15 respectively). Even though I was 28 at the time that did not seem to be an obstacle. A solid lifelong relationship was forged between our two families.

ROCHESTER SOARING CLUB

I think joining the Rochester Soaring Club (RSC) was number one on my priority list. Well, it might have been second to finding a job. Their fleet was not impressive; a Schweizer 2-22 and one of the monstrous TG-3's.

The club had picked up a custom from the world of sailing, which is to give endearing names to their boats. I think it's a charming custom and have been puzzled as to why the world of soaring never embraced this tradition. I can't believe it being much beyond anyone's imagination to come up with a fitting name for their elegant possession. The club had certainly come up with a fitting name for the TG-3; "Dyna-Soar." I really shouldn't pick on "Dyna-Soar", after all it was half of the fleet, and there were times it was actually possible to keep it in the air. I must add that it took more than thermaling know-how, it was also a physical challenge, especially when it was turbulent; two hands on the stick and you did well if you could last an hour. Nonetheless, it was flying and we were happy. The spin characteristics were not for the faint of heart. Warning of an impending spin was slight to non-existent, but when it did enter, all doubt was removed. Half the members who received spin training in the "Dyna-Soar" would never get back in it. This wasn't all bad as that left more glider accessibility for the Seymour's and me.

CAR-PULLEY TOWS

Our situation from Buffalo had changed dramatically. With no overtime at my new job, our budget was cut to pieces. It soon became clear that $4.00 tows were out of the question. Something had to be done. A winch would be perfect, but a winch meant a lot of money and work. Car tows seemed like the ideal compromise. It did not take long to convince Ed Seymour that this was a worthwhile endeavor to pursue. We promptly made a deep sheave pulley and bought 2000' of rope.

Not knowing any better, we started out with the wrong kind of rope, nylon. The idea was that with all the give in the rope it would make for nice smooth take-offs, and that was good enough. However, spectacular things happen whenever someone releases the rope under tension. This created knots of wondrous design and proportion, requiring endless hours to unravel. Of course there were times we had to resort to a pair of scissors.

It did not take long before we had to face reality and accept the fact that the nylon elasticity of the rope was OK during takeoffs, but that the aftermath of the release was more than we could handle. The nylon was replaced with polypropylene, which was a huge improvement. The afternoons were no longer spent untangling knots.

CROSS-COUNTRY FLYING

In spite of the impossibility of the situation, I remained obsessed with the idea of cross-country flying. Then I had a miraculous inspiration; why not build a set of rigging tools to ease the rigging of the TG-3? Then I could attend the upcoming Canadian soaring contest that was to be held in Brantford, Ontario.

I ended up entering the Canadian Nationals, in Kitchener, Ontario, with the club's glorious Schweizer 2-22. I never seemed to have problems using the club's ships during these excursions. The possibility of actually competing was obviously out of the question as the 2-22 was hardly a match for a 1-21, the Sky-Lark 3, and such. When the winners gave their speech, I was completely astounded to hear that they never got back down to release altitude once underway, whereas I never got back up to it. It was hard to believe that the flight they described was done on the same day. There is no way I could relate their distance and speed to my experience.

All my flights followed pretty much the same pattern. One climb after tow (because I was towed to a thermal), one glide to the next cloud arriving there at about 800' (with a field selected), hanging on by going around and around, and drifting from field to field in the desperate hope that I would eventually work my way back up again, which never happened.

Now of course by the time I landed, de-rigged in the field, and got on the road, all restaurants were closed so we missed dinner a few days. Yet Helga held up, in fine style and remarkably was ready to do the whole thing all over again the next day.

OWNING A GLIDER, FINALLY

Somewhere around this time I heard about a 1/3 ownership share being available in a glider; two guys were looking for a 3rd partner in a LK (Leister Kauffman). The only problem was the price of $500, and I really did not have the right to buy it because our bank account was minimal; but Helga wanted me to be happy and I was irresponsible enough to do it. The other two partners were Bob Barber and Norm Gowin.

Now this LK looked fabulously streamlined to us, but it had its draw backs. First off, it was designed and built for the army which meant designed and built to be assembled just once. Consequently, rigging the thing was a two-hour ordeal of hard labor – but nothing could quell our enthusiasm. No matter how you looked at it, it certainly was a much better choice to take to a contest than a TG-3.

GOLD C

Shortly thereafter, Don Ryon joined the club and he purchased one of the first Schweizer 1-26's. In short order he allowed the Seymour's and I to fly the 1-26 whenever we liked. Gliding took on a whole new dimension. Since I could fly the 1-26 while my partner flew the LK, we both set out for our Gold C flight.

As it turned out, my parents were visiting and crewed for me along with Helga. I thought I was going to drive my dad crazy because I refused to take and aero tow. My dad was willing to pay for the tow but that was not the point; it was a matter of principal to take a car tow, and of course I got away![2] I met up with Norm at Syracuse where he thought he might as well land as it started to look hopeless to make the distance. I did not see it that way; as long as I was in the air there was hope, and what-do-you-know, I made the 189 miles! This flight stands as the longest flight in a 1-26 in New York State.

This is as far as Kai got in writing his memoirs. He died of cancer on May 23, 2011.

---

[2] Kai Gertsen holds US Diamond # 25, the first Diamond badge earned entirely east of the Mississippi and launched by car tows only.

Seymours, 1961

Charlie, New Castle, 1986

Kai & Helga, with Ed's Ka-6, June 1986

Kai & John Seymour

Kai in Ka-6

Kai, Helga & Libelle

Kai with LK on trailer

Gertsens and Seymours

Chapter 6

*For 60 years, Kai flew many long- distance flights,
contests and records. "You don't get
anywhere flying in circles", he used to say.
His unrelenting optimism, flying skills, and inner steel,
earned him the name " Iron Man".*

*Of his many articles and essays, we selected three: a report
on his 500K diamond badge flight, (he holds US #25), the historic
1990 New Castle 1000K, and a land -out story.*

*These reports will give you insight into his in-flight decision making,
his eye for beauty, and his sense of humor.*

DIAMOND IN THE EAST

On May 4, 1963, three weeks after my first free distance diamond attempt, which came to an end at Hyde Airport, Clinton, Maryland after I covered a distance of 269 miles, I was ready for another try.

A check with the weather bureau at Rochester indicated good prefrontal conditions, the region being dominated by warm, unstable air, with a cold front expected to move through the area by evening. Meanwhile, we could expect the wind to remain from the WSW at 20 mph. Cumulus was expected to form with bases at 4000' and tops to 20-25,000', indicating a good possibility of over-development.

A good forecast and I was not to be disappointed.

As my crew and tow-car driver, Rex Wells, and I approached Dansville Airport it became apparent by the cumulus already dotting the sky, that we were late. Apparently one always is on the good days!

Feverishly the KA-6 was rigged and washed, tow-rope unwound, and other preparations made, while the cumulus were maturing rapidly. At 11:15 a.m. I instructed my devoted crew to "head for Boston", and 5 minutes later he dragged me off the ground.

From the 750' tow I reached the ridge, east of the airport, with 500' in hand. After polishing the ridge for a few minutes, a 200ft/min thermal was contacted and Dansville soon lowered away. My rate of climb did not correspond with the vigorously forming cu's surrounding me. At 3000' msl I got impatient and headed out on course. During the following three quarters of an hour, conditions improved steadily and at Penn Yan, the cu's were forming in "streets", consisting of 3 to 4 cu's closely spaced, netting 4-500ft/min rate of climb. Fortunately the cloud base was not as forecast, but a delightful 7000' msl. However, I soon discovered that it was futile to operate near cloud base, as the haze made it impossible to evaluate the conditions ahead. When first encountering these conditions I had found nothing but some high debris associated with considerable "down." Feeling quite foolish about the whole thing, I had eased off the speed and snuck away, looking for something more substantial. This bit of fumbling did not place me in too serious trouble as the "streets" were not too far apart and no great amount of altitude was lost in jogging over to the next one. From Penn Yan I proceeded without circling; only regulating the speed in accordance with varying rates of climb or descent.

Unfortunately, this supreme living was all too short. It ended abruptly at Cayuga Lake, where the sky went to pieces. No cumulus was in sight to the north or east. The only area that was showing any signs of convection was at the southern tip of the lake where some well-developed cu's were brewing. Promptly I headed south, along the eastern shore of the lake. Four miles north of Ithaca I reached the nearest cu'. Approaching the cloud base it became evident that the immediate area was overdeveloping so the thermal I had was squeezed to 7300' msl, which I used to reach the - by now - improving conditions to the north.

From here on it became quite a game to out-run and out-wit the rapidly changing conditions. Once an area became active it would overdevelop with amazing speed, form a complete overcast, and become utterly useless. Things were going great until I nearly got over-run by a vast, deflated cumulus nimbus about 10 miles NE of Richfield Springs. Reaching the sunshine with 1300' above ground, I was getting concerned. To land at this stage of the game, 150 miles out at 2 pm, would have been frustrating. Fortunately, this was not to be; a thermal, triggered by a gentle southward slope, saved the day. Twenty minutes later I was back at 6000', heading north-east, closely pursued by the grey monster from whose grasp I had just barely escaped. This brought me over Gloversville, at the southern tip of the Adirondacks, from which point I was able to resume an easterly heading.

At 3.30pm, over North Bennington, Vermont, I was facing the Green Mountains. Now what? To attempt to skirt south around the mountains with a 25kt WSW breeze to cope with would most certainly be like throwing my 500km out the window. The thought of landing here was absurd. Bewildered, I gazed at the wooded, mountainous terrain ahead. The 6600' indicated on the altimeter was rather deceiving as the mountains here rise to over 3000' in places. I finally concluded, however, that this was no time to quit and cautiously tiptoed toward the nearest cu. I then experienced a few thrilling moments as I encountered the downdraft that surrounded the cu I was aiming at. A stolen glance in the direction of the last available fields behind me confirmed my suspicion that I had now passed the point of no-return. I was somewhat relieved when at 5400' I entered the safety of a thermal which was good for a 400ft/min climb. While grinding around I was marveling at the spectacular scenery. It was rather hair-raising to watch the hostile terrain all the way around; nothing but densely wooded mountains as far as I could see, except for a few desolate summits where the naked rock was kept exposed by the constant winds.

After reaching cloud base at 6800', course was set for the next cu, which development I had been watching intensively during my previous climb. Three thermals later the excitement was over as the first cultivated fields, west of Keene, N.H., came in sight and the perilous terrain had been crossed without incident as I managed to remain above 5000' msl.

Arriving over Keene's Dillant Hopkins Airport at 3400', it looked as if the flight might end there, as the sky once again over-developed. The once active cumulus was hanging motionless, all blended together, shading the entire area. Here luck was with me again. Over the airport I found some "zero" lift and was able to hang on while the debris burned off and things got going again. Back at 6800', course was set for Peterborough, where at 5 pm the best thermal of the day got me to 8700' at the rate of 6-700ft/min under one isolated cu. This was a victorious moment as I knew I had the 500km in the bag. The magic circle was passed at Nashua at 5:21 pm with 6400' at which point the map was consulted for an airport within reach, on the shores of the Atlantic. Plum Island Airport at Newburyport seemed a good choice. Over Haverhill I worked the last thermal of the day for 800', which I knew I didn't need. This got me to Newburyport with 3400' to spare. The extra altitude was used for a picture taking tour along the shore and a short dash out over the Atlantic, taking pictures to prove that I had really done it! Having finished my sightseeing tour, I returned to land at the airport at 6:03 pm after a 6 hours and 42 minutes flight, covering a distance of 350 miles.*

*Note: Helga and their daughters remember that he used to say "had I known they had seen me approach from the Atlantic, I would have gotten out of the glider speaking Danish!"

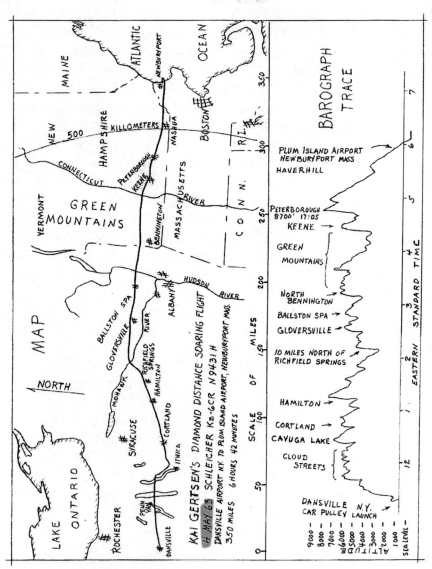

MAP AND BAROGRAPH TRACE OF KAI GERTSEN'S DIAMOND DISTANCE SOARING FLIGHT

APPALACHIAN MISSION

The adrenalin was already starting to flow. It was 8 o'clock, the evening of September 16, 1990, the end of the first contest day of the Region 4 South Championships. We were in the briefing room of the Blue Ridge Soaring Society's clubhouse, better known as "the White House." The somewhat early pilots' meeting for Day 2 was prompted by the forecast calling for a cold front to pass through the area overnight and northwest winds of 15 knots, gusting to 24, for the next day. Karl Striedieck was standing in front of the floor to ceiling relief map of the Appalachian range, pointing with a broom handle. "Now when you make the transition here, get high, because there are no places to land. Watch out for wave suppression on this stretch," and so on…

He was addressing a very attentive group of about 20 pilots aspiring to join the elite 1000K Club. The proposed task started with a run southwest, down the ridge from New Castle to Big Walker Tunnel, where I-77 cuts through the mountain; then north through four states up to Bedford, Pennsylvania (the turn point being the fire tower on the hill just south of town), then all the way back down to Big Walker Quarry, next to the tunnel, before coming back home, a distance of 1008 km (627 mile). The sailplanes were already rigged and ballasted with water and tied down for the night, except for Bravo India (alias Kilo India). I decided we could just as well rig in the morning, since the "24" was not able to carry water as the electrically activated valves were inoperative.

Poking our heads out of the tent at 6 am the next morning, we were somewhat discouraged by the dead calm, but by 7 am we had the "24" rigged and ready, just in case. At the 8:15 am pilots' meeting, at the front of the grid, the wind had perked up and was indeed conforming to the forecast. The longest task ever declared at a contest was on.

Immediately after going through the gate, at 9:12 am, I was on the ridge heading south. The trip to the tunnel proved to be an easy run. Near the first turn, Striedieck streaked by going in the opposite direction having already made the turn. "How would you like some of my water? $50,- per gallon." Weird sense of humor, I thought, bobbing along with my 6.5 lb wing loading.

The first 128 miles were in the bag by 10:30 am. Now, back near New Castle, it was time to transit to the main ridge. This turned out to be considerable less difficult than anticipated. A cu over Maggie ridge was good for 6 knots to 4,000 feet. Nearing cloud base, I shifted upwind and the thermal blended right into a wave with no change in the rate of climb. Well above the cu's, at 7,200 feet, the course was set directly to Covington. The visibility was superb and the scenery magnificent, with mountains stretching to the horizon in all directions beneath a layer of scattered cumulus. At Covington I caught up with Ed Byars and Karl Striedieck. As Ed and I hoisted ourselves up, Karl struck out and shortly thereafter announced, in a matter of fact tone of voice, "I'm in trouble. The ridge by this lake isn't working. I am low and will probably be landing shortly." Fascinating! As far as we could see, the lake was surrounded by forest. Thus encouraged, we proceeded with caution. As we came closer, a field large enough for a crash landing came into view and a stretch of mud flats could be seen on the other side. Fortunately, we never found out what his choice would have been, for in the next message he informed us he was now climbing at 1 knot.

Nearing Mountain Grove, we should now be upon the ridge. I have always envisioned, as I am certain some of our friends from Texas have, the ridge used on these flights to be well defined and fairly uninterrupted. Not so! The landscape ahead was helter-skelter and soon the radio came alive with all sorts of inquiries. "Which one is the ridge?" "Am I in the right place over here?" "At this bowl, do I go right or left?" The correct choice was not at all obvious, it being a relatively low ridge, downwind of a much higher slope, and culminating in a steep V shaped valley. People ahead had been reporting the ridge to be getting soft and there had been some concern, at the pilots' meeting, about the possibility of the wind being too northerly for this portion of the ridge to be working. Therefore it was with some trepidation that I ventured down on the ridge. I was soon breathing easier though as the ridge was indeed working, so I tucked it in tight and poured on the coal.

Progress was now being made at a high rate of speed, flashing along the tortuous landscape, with the ever changing scenery getting even more spectacular. At one stretch, we flew along a 100 feet high vertical rock face. Further on, the shale rock had through the millennia been pushed up into a continuous vertical wall which zigzagged up and down along the ridge crest, like some scaled down version of the Chinese wall. Blasting along at 100 knots, about 50 feet from trees and rocks, I contemplated what a spectacular IMAX movie this would make, feeling extremely grateful for being one of the very few in this world ever to experience this kind of adventure.

Approaching the town of Scherr, West Virginia, we were upon the dreaded Knobblies. This is where the ridge disperses into a scattering of pebble sized mounds. It was time to get some respectable altitude. A considerable amount of valuable time was wasted here, primarily due to my judgment being hampered by the vivid memory of last year's flight with Roy McMaster from Harris Hill. On that occasion I had ventured into the Knobblies at low altitude and almost scared myself to death. Consequently, I now overreacted and got off the ridge too soon and stayed high for too long. That's when I discovered that I should have heeded Helga's sound advice to dress warm, for here I was in my T-shirt with temperatures well below freezing. Fortunately, the time available to ponder my level of discomfort was brief. The sky was now 5/10 cu's with 6 knot climbs everywhere so it didn't take long to get across the Knobblies and the Bedford gap. It was time to press down on the ridges again. Then came another safety call from Karl. "Go easy at Snowy Mountain. It's a little soft there." Upon arriving I immediately recognized the spot where I almost landed the Discus last year. This time, approaching with caution, I got by without incident. The remaining run to Bedford was straight-forward and the fire tower was photographed at 14:31 hrs. Now all that remained was to repeat everything in reverse.

With a quartering tail wind, the ground speed on the trip south was considerably faster. Near Keyser, I met up with Ed Byars again. We cranked up together in preparation for our crossing of the Knobblies. Once again he left me behind, the dry "24" being no match for his fully ballasted Discus. Back on the trees, we once more skimmed by the Chinese wall and the imposing rock escarpments. At Mountain Grove, the lake in the woods loomed ahead and it was decision time again. I contemplated the strategy of crossing over and flying the main ridge to I-77, then following I-77 downwind to the tunnel. It seemed like a reasonable plan but the main ridge, at this point, was not that well defined. I had no idea what was on the other side. It was getting late. The cu's were now short-lived wisps and the entire area was all forest. I half-heartedly started out in that direction but, after a couple of thermals, elected to ease my mind and headed for Covington instead. It should be a simple matter to get a thermal off the ridge there, for the remaining 22 miles to New Castle.

Twenty minutes after arriving at Covington, it was becoming obvious that a considerable amount of luck would be required to get back home, let alone completing the task. The ridge leading to the tunnel originates at New Castle, where it parallels the Maggie ridge which lies one mile to the west. The valley between the two ridges is located approximately 1000 feet above the town of New Castle, where the two ridges come together in the shape of a bowl with a gap above the town. To connect with the ridge one must arrive at New Castle with 1500 feet to spare. I finally accepted the fact that the Covington ridge was simply not producing anymore thermals that day. Consequently, when a mist dome appeared over the valley, I went for it. Ed Kilbourne's song, "Just one more climb" says it all. It was now twenty minutes past five. If I could milk enough altitude out of this thermal to arrive at New Castle with enough height to get through the gap and onto the ridge, it might still be possible to complete the task. My emotional disposition reached another low as the thermal stopped short of getting me the required altitude. With all hope of completing the task gone, I reluctantly left what surely must have been the very last thermal in the sky. Well at least I should be able to get to the airport. I transmitted this state of affairs to Helga to ease her mind; at which point John Seymour immediately got on the radio; "Keep coming Bravo India. The ridge to the tunnel is really cooking." That was just the moral support I needed. Maybe there was still hope, but I had to admit, it looked marginal. Then John was back with more encouragement. "Don't forget you have a 44 glide ratio on that machine. You can't miss." Halfway back to New Castle, miracle of miracles, I stumbled into another thermal and that clinched it. At twenty minutes to six, I streaked across the town of New Castle, through the gap and onto the ridge. Now I was racing the sun. There was 128 miles to go and the sun would be setting at 19:10 pm. Another nagging question crept in. Would the wind subside before I could get back? This distressing prospect plagued me the rest of the way.

I was relieved to round the last turn point and turn my back to the setting sun, which had been blinding me all the way from New Castle. Now it greatly enhanced the beauty of the scenery, deepening the shadows, accentuating the mountains and the steeply sloped fields. Void of thermals, the ridge lift was now smooth sustaining at 80 knots. My worry that the wind might quit turned out to be unfounded. At last, within easy reach of the finish line, I dove over the backside of the ridge. What a ride! I crossed the finish line 4 minutes before sunset and shortly after rolled up by the trailer, where I was greeted by a welcoming committee consisting of Helga, John and Karl. A fitting conclusion to my 10 hour odyssey.

There were a total of 17 completions, including one guest. The total distance flown by all pilots nearly equals half the way around the world! We are all indebted to John Seymour and Karl Striedieck; not only do they know the terrain like the back of their hand and have the savvy to know when the weather is right, they also had the courage to send us rookies on this mind boggling mission. John and Karl's speed was 86.1 and 79.7 mph, respectively. Yours truly was the slowest at 63.5 mph. But I really didn't care. I was the happiest man in the world.

```
1990 REGION 4 SOUTH SOARING CONTEST                    17 SEPTEMBER 1990
              NEW CASTLE, VIRGINIA                         ** OFFICIAL **

DAY  2  SPEED  626.8 MILES  (1008.7 KM)                    15 METER CLASS
BIG WALKER TUNNEL, BEDFORD FIRE TOWER, BIG WALKER QUARRY, NEW CASTLE
```

PL	PILOT	CN	SAILPLANE	DIST	SPEED	SCORE	CUM	SCORE	PEN
1	SEYMOUR, JOHN	SM	ASW-20B	626.8	86.14	1000	1	1864	
9	NIXON, HANK	UH	ASW-20C	626.8	74.82	869	2	1719	
2	JURADO, ALFONSO	E9	ASW-20	626.8	78.46	911	3	1642	
3	COLE, DAVID	A	ASW-20C	626.8	77.90	904	4	1591	
13	WHITTEMORE, BOB	WB	ASW-20	154.3		813	5	1588	@
10	SAVORY, WILLIAM	9	VENTUS C	626.8	74.13	861	6	1501	
8	SMITH, PENN	2P	LS-6A	626.8	75.04	871	7	1489	
14	STOIA, JIM	PA	LS-6	118.3		813	8	1387	@
7	LAUCK, TONY	TL	VENTUS-C	626.8	75.20	873	9	1322	
6	WELLES, TIM	R6	ASW-20	626.8	75.63	878	10	1277	
4	WELLES, DAVE	18	SGS 1-35	626.8	76.19	884	11	1212	
5	MURRAY, JOHN	29	ASW-20B	626.8	75.65	878	12	1182	
14	SMITH, MIKE	XM	ASW-20	118.3		813	13	1175	@
11	JACKSON, BOB	RJ	ASW-20	626.8	74.09	860	14	1008	
12	GREGG, JASON	YB	VENTUS	626.8	70.11	814	15	962	
14	MESSNER, BOB	8U	VENTUS-B	118.3		813	16	841	@
14	NELSON, RICHARD	DQ	ASW-20C	118.3		813	17	813	@
18	GREER, ALAN	A3	VENTUS B/T	0.0		813	18	813	@
19	NADLER, DAVE	YO	LS-6B	DNC		0	19	275	

```
DAY  2  SPEED  626.8 MILES  (1008.7 KM)                    STANDARD CLASS
BIG WALKER TUNNEL, BEDFORD FIRE TOWER, BIG WALKER QUARRY, NEW CASTLE
```

PL	PILOT	CN	SAILPLANE	DIST	SPEED	SCORE	CUM	SCORE	PEN
1	STRIEDIECK, KARL	KS	ASW-24	626.8	79.68	1000	1	2000	
3	BYARS, ED	ED	DISCUS-A	626.8	68.22	856	2	1690	
4	GERTSEN, KAI	BI	ASW-24	626.8	63.54	797	3	1439	
2	GOOD, JOHN	FS	DG-300	626.8	74.72	938	4	1099	
5	BYARS, GUY FORD	11	LS-4	118.3		796	5	957	@

```
# = PENALTY APPLIED                    T = POST TIME LIMIT NOT MET

@ = SCORES CORRECTED FOR THOSE NOT FLYING 1000 KM TASK
```

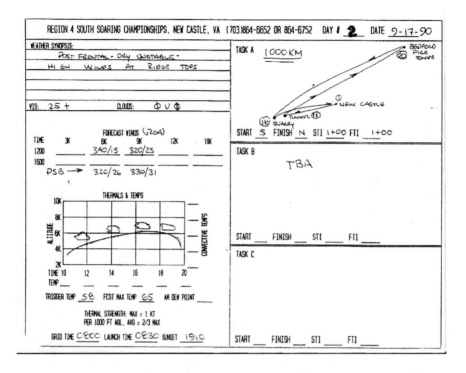

Ridge runners 18 September 1990

MUTINY

Another great task in those days was the "Free Distance." This task also brought the crews into the action and allowed them to fully appreciate the country side, and share in the adventure. During the 1964 Canadian Nationals in Regina, Saskatchewan, we had the pleasure of being assigned a Free Distance task.

It was one beautiful day and I thought we could go on forever, but at 230 miles out, coming upon the endless swamps and woodlands of Northern Manitoba, I concluded that the reasonable thing to do was to land while there still was a field to land in.

It turned out everyone else did the same thing except for a young fellow by the name of Roy Gray. Apparently having the "right stuff" and being young enough to believe himself to be invincible, he fearlessly continued on into oblivion. Eventually, by some miracle, he did find some sort of clearing to land in, but it took him 24 hours to get to a telephone. The retrieve, necessitating a vast detour via Winnipeg, turned out to be about 700 miles long. Needless to say, he won the day, hands down. Unfortunately he missed the next two contest days.

Meanwhile, I came back to earth near the town of St. Rose du Lac, Manitoba, on a humble farm run by a French speaking widow and her two teenage boys.

I always like to write down the directions for my crew prior to making the phone call back to the retrieve desk at headquarters. Looking for a place to rest my paper on, I finally abandoned the search for a suitable horizontal surface and scoured the walls for a fitting spot, but they turned out to be as thickly covered with grease as everything else. Then I watched with suppressed terror as dinner was being prepared. The mother was slapping hamburgers together with hands that looked like she had been digging up her great grandmother. I fervently hoped not to be invited, but of course, I was. I looked at the boys; they looked healthy enough and if they could survive this I convinced myself I could as well and gracefully accepted.

After dinner, the boys offered to show me around town. So we climbed into their antiquated relic of a pick-up truck and headed for town. As it were, the town consisted of a church, a firehouse and a beer parlor. After the third pass by the beer parlor, I finally got the hint (I was a little slow), but I protested, explaining that I always wait for my wife by the roadside or the glider. They pointed out that with 300 miles to go she was not likely to get there anytime soon. That was a reasonable enough argument, but I emphasized that it would be strictly one beer only.

As we walked through the door I couldn't believe my eyes. There, at one of the tables, sat Peter Towsend, a fellow competitor. This was totally incredible. Keep in mind that in the days before radios, nobody had the slightest idea as to where everyone else was heading. As it were, he had landed just a couple of miles from where I wound up. So, naturally we had to swap stories. Now, you can hardly cover two great flights like that in the time of just one beer. Then after we finished Peter's and my round of beer we really could not be rude and turn down the boys offer to reciprocate. Well, next thing we knew we were having a fabulous time.

Meanwhile, Helga arrived at the farm. She was puzzled as to why I had not been out by the road waiting for her. When Helga asked the widow if she had any idea as to where I might be, she replied in a broad French accent "I think beer parlor." Helga replied that I definitely would not be at a beer parlor, more likely I was with the glider. "Oh no, I think beer parlor," the farm woman repeated but Helga insisted. Begrudged, the lady pointed to where she thought the glider was and Helga headed off in that direction.

By now it was pitch dark, and Helga inadvertently wound up driving down a cow path with a barbed wire fence on both sides. Unfortunately the cow path was a dead-end, and it was too narrow to turn the rig around. The only solution was to unhook the trailer, clock it around by hand and hitch it up again. I should point out that in those days during contests we lived in our station wagon, also referred to as the "Chevy Motel." Also, the contest area had been blessed with an extended draught and the ground consisted of ankle deep, fine dust that rose in great clouds with every footstep.

When Helga attempted to unhook the trailer she discovered that the hitch had been securely cemented with a mixture of dust and road oil, and strong measures were required to unhook this thing. A hefty hammer might do the job. But the hammer was stashed in the 50lb toolbox, securely stowed in the lower storage compartment below the suitcases and sleeping bags which by now were covered by a ¼ inch layer of dust, and the mosquitoes did their part to add to the misery. For Helga, the fun of this adventure was beginning to ebb.

Back at the beer parlor we were having a great time until Peter's crew walked in. My mind was still sharp enough to realize that if his crew was here, Helga couldn't be far behind. Time was of the essence, I simply had to get back to the glider before she arrived. I had to get out of here quick. Regrettably, I didn't even manage to get up from the table. Next thing I knew, the young fellow who turned up to help Helga walked in. Judging by his uneasy grin I concluded that Helga was probably not in a very good mood and would not be the least bit interested in hearing about my great flight. I was right, she did not look happy at all.

We managed to find the glider, take it apart and load it onto the trailer in close company of a million mosquitoes that did not seem at all hampered by the clouds of dust. When ready to go, I thought it would be appropriate for me to do my share. Slightly slurred, I offered to drive. "You are not fit to drive! Get in the back!" was her stern command. Obediently I crawled in, on top of the sleeping bags and suitcases, blissfully oblivious to the ¼ inch layer of dust, and passed out.

I regained consciousness as we rolled onto the airfield beneath beautiful morning cu's. In short order we all regrouped and began considering what might be an appropriate task for the day. Excitement was mounting; it was shaping up to be another great soaring day. At this point Helga spoke up, "I don't know and I don't care what you are doing today, but I am checking into a motel, have a bath and go to sleep!" I was completely flabbergasted. I could not believe it. This was completely *unreasonable*. Even the other crews were somewhat taken aback. This was not at all the quiet, easy going Helga, but it didn't take the other crews long to recover and follow her lead. This was outright *mutiny*! Now everybody was going to take a bath! I was totally baffled as to what could have brought this on. So, she had missed dinner for a couple of days, surely that was no reason to make such a fuss! I admit it had been a long drive yesterday but the day before had been a fairly short retrieve, a mere three hundred miles round trip. What had brought us to this sad state? A gorgeous soaring day was lost. What in the world could be the problem?

Moral of this story; by all means, *by any means*, stick to the one beer limit…

Helga preparing supper after a retrieve. LK on the right.

ENCORE

My Paradise

Eagerly I fling my slender craft into
The murky mist of a thunderous cloud.
I marvel at the boundless energy,
Accelerating me to breathtaking speed -
Up and up, to endless heights.

Absorbed by this monstrous creation,
Testing my endurance by relentless
Pounding of hail and gusts;
I struggle to keep my craft on even heel.

Reaching the top of that dark perilous
Stairway, I plunge out into sunburst brilliance
Which overpowering beauty
Is magnified by its staggering contrast
With the world just left behind.

From misty valleys far below
Columns of vapor blossoms into
Fantasy Mountains with deep crevices
And towering peaks, this could be a scene
From some unknown distant planet.

In the silent cockpit of my great white bird,
With unobstructed panoramic view,
I let all my senses feast on this abundance
Of beauty, in a state of ecstasy
I am suspended in my paradise.

- Kai Gertsen

These Appendices are publications written by Kai during the years he instructed at Harris Hill and Finger Lakes Soaring, NY. These instructional publications gained worldwide recognition and were adopted in many places as cross-country instructional materials.

APPENDIX 1

SPINNING

By Kai Gertsen

WHY SPIN TRAINING

Spinning is the biggest cause of gliding fatalities. Every year we lose a handful of our fellow glider pilots in this country to spin-ins. This is truly tragic, as I am certain these accidents would not occur if all pilots received adequate spin training. I know of several cases where spin training saved the day. Pilots who are not prepared are not likely to take proper action when the time comes.

In recent times we have had two spin accidents involving club members. One pilot did not survive, the other miraculously escaped injury, and two gliders were destroyed.

It is not only inexperienced, low time pilots who fall victim to this insidious killer. Pilots with thousands of hours have known to be caught unprepared.

A few years ago the soaring movement lost two very prominent and experienced pilots in a Nimbus 4. The accident was apparently due to miss handling of the controls during an inadvertent spin, causing the glider to enter an extreme nose down attitude resulting in the airspeed getting out of control. The glider exceeded the red line (Vne) and disintegrated. One of the pilots was a former National Soaring Champion, a record holder and had been a member of the US World Championship Team.

Although the FAA requirement is only for Stall and Spin Awareness Training (AC61-67B), not spin training, I firmly believe spin training should be mandatory for all glider pilots prior to solo. By the nature of our flying we are considerably more susceptible to inadvertent spins than power pilots, although they are not doing all that well either with 25% of fatalities in general aviation being attributable to spins.

It is imperative to be able to immediately recognize an incipient spin. Suppose you are preparing to join several other gliders in the pattern. You are busy trying to figure out what everyone else is going to do when all of a sudden the left wing drops. If you are a little fuzzy on the topic of spinning, my guess is your reaction would be to move the stick over to the right, to pick up the left wing, which only aggravates the situation, and then the nose drops. In a desperate attempt to avoid disaster, you immediately pull back on the stick. To your amazement the nose drops further and the downward motion of the left wing gathers momentum. As the ground is now rapidly approaching, you instinctively pull the stick all the way back in the corner. I will leave the next event in this sequence to your imagination. Don't let a similar scenario be your introduction to incipient spins.

To be meaningful, whatever spin training is done needs to take place in a glider with somewhat the same propensity to spinning, and require the same prompt correct response as any glider you are likely to fly. It is true that all gliders can spin, but some are more reluctant than others.

Attempting spin training in a glider such as a Schweizer 2-33 is counter-productive. Wallowing around in a 2-33 engaged in Herculean efforts to simulate a halfhearted spin entry will only serve to convince you that it is virtually impossible to spin a glider, and that spins are nothing to worry about, thus setting a deadly trap ready to be sprung when you least expect it.

One purpose of full spin training is to get familiar with the 'feel' of spinning, so that the tendency to panic in a real spin situation is greatly reduced. A low, inadvertent spin does not give a pilot unfamiliar with spins time to work out what is happening before hitting the ground.

Very few pilots recover from inadvertent low level spins.

Be assured that if you fly gliders long enough, sooner or later you will experience an inadvertent spin entry, and probably when you least expect it. Better be prepared.

WHEN ARE WE MOST AT RISK

Most spin accidents occur while turning onto final from a pattern flown too low (which unfortunately, is a common practice at Harris Hill). Typically, encouraged by the close proximity to the ground when turning final, the angle of bank is minimized, and more rudder is progressively being applied in an effort to get lined up with the runway while pulling the nose up in an effort to conserve altitude. There you have the perfect set-up for a spin; this classic scenario has brought many pilots to a bad end. This maneuver, spin entry from a flat skidding turn, should be practiced until the resulting incipient spin can be recognized immediately, and recovered from with minimal loss of altitude.

Another classic; attempting to thermal at low levels especially if using shallow banked turns and minimum airspeed.

Turbulence can cause a glider to stall at a significantly higher airspeed than in stable conditions. I have experienced incipient spins from tight turns at 60kts while thermaling off a ridge in windy and turbulent conditions.

Distraction is another culprit. Whenever you are faced with a distraction your are at increased risk, as when your attention is diverted away from the task of flying the glider during a challenging off-airport landing.

WHAT IS AN INCIPIENT SPIN

An incipient spin is that portion of a spin from the time the glider stalls and rotation starts, until the spin becomes fully developed.

WHAT IS A SPIN

A spin is basically a stable condition in which one wing is stalled and the other wing remains flying.

If the glider stalls asymmetrically due to yaw, air turbulence or non-symmetrical wing profiles (e.g. rigging, aileron deflection, bugs), then one wing will stall before the other and drop.

The angle of attack of the dropping wing increases, causing further loss of lift and an increase in drag. The up-going wing experiences the reverse.

The difference in drag between the upper and lower wings causes the nose to yaw in the direction of the down-going wing. This results in the lower wing going even slower and becoming more stalled.

Unless the glider is un-stalled, it continues to rotate automatically (Autorotation) with the stalled wing inboard, rolling, yawing and pitching simultaneously in a steeply descending helical path.

The spin is characterized by a nose-down rapid rotation of the glider, a very high rate of descent, and lack of response to ailerons and elevator.

THAT IS A FLAT SPIN

A flat spin is characterized by near level pitch and bank attitude with the spin axis near the center of gravity.

INTRODUCTION TO SPINS

First let me say that there is no reason to fear spins. Providing the specific type of glider is certified for spinning, it is perfectly safe and not nearly as terrifying as you might have imagined. The only reason you may have to fear spins is if you have not had any training or you have failed to stay current.

You should not, under any circumstance practice spins without first being checked out by an instructor.

Your initial introduction to spinning may be a demonstration by the instructor while you have your hands and feet off the controls. For some, the first spin can be an intense experience. On a few occasions the student has been known to get a little uptight and the instructor had difficulties overpowering the student's grip on the stick.

It is not unlikely that you may experience some disorientation, which is perfectly normal during the initial check-out. Another reason this exercise is so important.

INCIPIENT SPIN RECOGNITION AND RECOVERY

A spin entry is recognizable by a sudden wing drop with an abrupt yaw toward the falling wing, the yaw being caused by the wing stalling. It is distinctly different from a wing drop caused by turbulence, and with some practice, can easily learned to be recognized.

At the incipient stage, a forward movement of the stick will un-stall the inboard wing and the glider will instantly recover. In most cases merely relaxing the back-pressure will do the trick. If the pilot fails to respond immediately the nose will drop as well.

It is the failure of the pilot to move the stick forward when the wing drops and the nose is going down that allows the glider to spin.

It used to be that the recovery procedure taught was to pick up the wing by the application of opposite rudder. Now, we know better. Applying opposite rudder at this stage can cause the glider to enter a spin in the other direction. Remember, a glider will spin in the direction of rudder deflection.

Conversely, if you should fail to recognize the wing drop as an incipient spin, and attempt to pick-up the wing with the ailerons, which is a natural reaction, the result will be a full spin entry. The reason for this is that the aileron on the stalled wing will move down which effectively increases the angle of attack, thus aggravating the stall.

RECOVERY FROM A FULLY DEVELOPED SPIN

1. Apply Full Opposite Rudder.
2. Neutralize Elevator and Ailerons
3. Ease the Stick Gradually Forward till Rotation Stops.
4. Neutralize the Rudder After Rotation stops.
5. Gently Pull Out of the Recovery Dive.

The crucial action is to move the stick forward to un-stall the glider even though the nose is dropping or pointing steeply downwards. It is the inability of pilots to take this action when the nose drops unexpectedly which results in stalling and spinning accidents.

When applying opposite rudder you will notice considerably more force on the pedals is required than usual. This could lead you to think that the instructor is interfering but it is more likely to be due to the increased air pressure on the rudder. Be sure you apply <u>full</u> rudder deflection.

Do not pause between step 1 and 2. Some flight manuals recommend the elevator and ailerons be neutralized at the same time opposite rudder is applied. In fact, the sequence could be reversed.

Avoid moving the stick forward further than required, as this causes excessive pitch down. In the old days students were taught to 'push the stick forward', which is really the wrong term. This often resulted in the student doing just that, with far too much vigor causing the glider to go beyond vertical once the rotation had stopped. This we could get away with back then as the post WW II gliders we used, such as the TG-3, was blessed with an enormous amount of drag. To-day's sleek designs are less forgiving; building up speed at an alarming rate once rotation stops and the glider is aimed at the ground. Remember whenever you are at high speed keep a firm grip on the stick.

Notice that ailerons are not used in recovery. To recover from a spin the inboard wing must be unstalled. Applying opposite aileron will only aggravate the stall and keep the glider spinning. Do not use the ailerons in an effort to raise the inboard wing.

When autorotation stops, immediately neutralize the rudder. If the rudder is 'held in' too long and the stick too far back the glider will almost always violently flip over and spin in the other direction. Because of the abrupt and unpleasant gyrations, this maneuver is seldom demonstrated. This is a common occurrence during spin-ins. The glider is seen to recover from the initial spin only to immediately flip over and spin in the other direction with no hope of recovery, as by this time the hapless pilot is running out of time and altitude. These accidents are solely attributable to a lack of familiarity with spins.

Once the rotation has stopped, the objective is to bring about a gradual recovery with minimum height loss, 'G' loads and airspeed build up. To prevent needless height loss, prompt control input is vital, but it must be smooth. You may find some who advocates having your hand on the airbrake lever in case the speed gets away from you, but this is not a good idea. When used as speed limiting, the airbrakes must be extended <u>before</u> the speed gets away. (See section on spiral dives, page 5)

HEIGHT LOSS

The height loss in the first second is 30 feet, the 2nd second 50-60 feet, and the third second 80-90 feet. The rate of descend once the spin is fully developed is about 100 feet per second or 70 MPH. In a modern two-seater trainer, the rate of rotation is in the order of 4 seconds per revolution.

Height loss in the recovery dive is in the order of about 150 feet the first second, 250 feet the 2nd second, and then increasing to 400 feet per second.

When combining the height loss during spinning with the loss of height during the recovery dive, then the height loss after the first 180° of rotation will be close to 300ft, certainly not something to try while turning from base to final.

After 360° of rotation total height loss will be in the order of 550ft. Two revolutions will use up about 750ft.

RECOVERY FROM A FLAT SPIN

With the center of gravity far enough back the glider may spin flat, from which it may not be possible to recover. Full forward stick may not get the nose down enough to get the inboard wing flying.

In case you forget to remove the tail dolly prior to take-off, it is imperative to maintain extra flying speed after release, to preclude any possibility of stalling. Incidentally, should you ever get airborne with the tail dolly on, do not release immediately. Wait till you get some reasonable altitude, say at least 1500ft., this gives you time to settle down and prepare a conservative pattern. Some have been known to release at the end of the runway and crash; no need for that.

In the unlikely event that you should ever encounter a flat spin and full forward stick has no effect, moving the stick rhythmically back and forth to get the fuselage oscillating may briefly pitch the fuselage down far enough to un-stall the inboard wing.

In some gliders spinning with flaps in the 'landing setting' is, for structural reasons strictly prohibited. If any attempt is made to employ the flaps to assist recovery use extreme caution.

EFFECT OF CONTROLS

At spin entry and during a fully developed spin the glider's reaction to aileron and elevator control inputs are reversed from normal; sure signs of a spin. Moving the stick back will cause the nose pitch down. Moving the stick to the opposite side of the low wing will cause it to drop faster.

Hence, at spin entry, moving the stick to the opposite side in an effort to raise the wing, and pulling back on the stick to raise the nose will assure a full spin entry. In a fully developed spin holding the stick back in the opposite corner will hold the glider in the spin. Unfortunately, this is the intuitive response, and many have done so in a desperate attempt to recover, all the way down.

For the most part, the rate of rotation, degree of nose down pitch, and airspeed are determined by the characteristics of the glider and the position of the center of gravity. However, the position of the ailerons can have some effects on pitch and roll oscillations, the rate of spin, and degree of pitch and bank. The affects, good or bad, will be unique to each glider. Better to keep the ailerons centered.

CAN ALL TYPE OF GLIDERS SPIN

All gliders will enter a spin given the right conditions. Turbulence can cause a glider to stall at a significantly higher airspeed than in stable conditions. I have experienced incipient spins from tight turns at 60kts while thermaling off a ridge in windy and turbulent conditions.

Any glider will also spin if sufficiently provoked and /or with the center of gravity near the aft limit. Some will recover shortly after entry, e.g. after one or two revolutions, even with the stick back in the corner. The spin will then transition into a spiral dive. Gliders which are reluctant to spin may well enter a spiral dive immediately following the incipient phase.

Other gliders such as the Schweizer 1-26 and 1-34 can enter a spin inadvertently, and will continue spinning until correct recover procedure is applied.

There are variations between gliders, and you should always get yourself acquainted with the spin and recovery characteristics of every glider you fly, as soon as possible. Not only are there variations between gliders, but spinning characteristics can be influenced by the configuration.

Flaps and their effects vary from glider to glider. In general, lowering the flaps will substantially encourage spins, as will an extended landing gear if located forward of the CG. The best example is the ASW-20, which is reluctant to spin with neutral or negative flaps, but spins like a top with gear down and landing flap. Warning - in some gliders, spinning in the landing flap setting is strictly prohibited. Always check the flight manual for operating limitations.

EFFECTS OF THE CENTER OF GRAVITY

A trainer such as the Schweizer 2-33 may be impossible to spin in spite of extreme spin provoking control positions, when flown with two people on board. However when flown solo, it may be susceptible to spinning. Keep in mind that in most two-seaters the rear seat is generally in front of the center of gravity. Consequently, the center of gravity is further back when the glider is flown solo than it is when the rear seat is also occupied.

With the CG in the middle of the range it generally takes about a second for the autorotation to stop, should the CG be near the rear limit it may take two or three seconds. If the CG is beyond the aft limit, the glider may spin flat (see section on recovery from flat spins, page 4).

SPINS VS. SPIRAL DIVES

A spin may transition into a spiral dive at any time without any input on your

117

part. It is crucial to be able to immediately recognize when a spin transitions to a spiral dive, as the recovery procedure is totally different. Fortunately for us, the spiral dive presents us with one clue that is a dead giveaway – the airspeed. While spinning, the airspeed indicator will show a low and /or flickering airspeed. Conversely, in a spiral dive the airspeed will build up an alarming rate, which is another reason instantaneous recognition is vital.

In a spiral dive –

1. The speed increases rapidly.
2. The controls feel heavy and are effective.
3. 'G' forces increase if the stick is held or moved back.
4. The rate of rotation is markedly slower than when spinning.

To avoid excessive loads, when recovering from a spiral dive always level the wings first before attempting to slow down. Level the wings using coordinated ailerons and rudder. Avoid pulling out and rolling level at the same time – the stresses on the glider can be extremely high.

Do not use the airbrakes to slow down. Most airbrakes are designed to be speed limiting, typically to limit the speed in dives of less than 45°, they are not intended to be <u>opened</u> at high speed. If the speed is very high it is better to slow down by pulling out without using the airbrakes.

Some of the reasons for avoiding opening the airbrakes at very high speeds are –
1. The forces on the airbrakes will be excessive and they will most certainly slam open violently when unlocked.
2. There will probably be damage done to the airbrake mechanism. This damage may make it impossible to close the airbrakes, at any speed.
3. More significantly, the redistribution of the loads on the wings due to opening the brakes at high speed may cause structural damage.

Aside from the dangers of opening the airbrakes at high speeds, be aware that you may not be able to close them, even at moderate high speeds. On one type of glider the airbrakes cannot be closed at speeds over 65kts.

WHY PRACTICE SPINS

Practice has two prime purposes - the more often seen, the sooner recognized, and only through practice is it possible to cultivate the correct response to become intuitive, which it must be to enable a pilot to recover from a low level spin entree.

It also takes practice to enable the pilot to know how far to move the stick to get an immediate recovery without causing an excessive nose down pitch, resulting in an extra height loss of several hundred feet or worse. A timely respond is also crucial; even a one second delay will cost 100 ft. Only practice will enable the pilot to immediately move the stick forward by just the right amount for a minimum height loss recovery.

Another part of the recovery which typically needs to be worked on, is the recovery dive. Only through practice can we learn the right amount of control input needed to minimize height loss, 'G' loads, and airspeed.

Spinning is one of those maneuvers that many of us tend to neglect after the initial check out, which may be one of the reasons why it remains such a high contributor to serious accidents.

Satisfactory demonstration of a spin entry and recovery during a mentally well-rehearsed and prepared exercise at a comfortable altitude does not guarantee immediate and correct action when encountering a completely unexpected spin, especially at low altitude. When aimed straight at the ground we are faced with a strong urge to apply opposite aileron and haul back on the stick, which, of course, will only serve to seal our doom.

Here are excerpts from a report by a British instructor:

"P2 was a young Bronze badge pilot on a check flight. Confidently pulling up and rolling into a thermal at about 3000ft, he reset the flaps but did not fully engage the flap lever in its détente slot. Before I could point this out the lever sprang out, the flaps went up and the wing already down dropped away as did the nose. He reacted instantaneously – putting the stick in the opposite corner!

Knowing we were clear of other traffic, it seemed fortuitously appropriate to leave him to recover (aircraft and self-esteem) but, despite entreaties from the back seat, the controls remained crossed until self-preservation instincts overcame tutorial motivation and I took over to recover (below 1500ft).

Back on the ground, his record showing no problems with pre-solo spin training, he said it was the unexpectedness of the spin which 'completely phased' him and volunteered that, alone, he most likely would have spun to the ground. Later he demonstrated spin and recovery quite satisfactorily but it was of course the usual training set piece performance for which by then he was mentally rehearsed and prepared."

We need to practice spins until the correct recovery control input becomes intuitive. Only then will we be totally prepared. If you have to think about it, you'll probably run out of time.

Here is another area that needs attention. As the spinning characteristics vary from one type of glider to another, it's a good idea to check out the spinning characteristics on one of the first flights when transitioning to a different type. Also, any modification you make to your present glider may very well make it behave like a different type and it will behoove you to treat it accordingly. Fitting your glider with winglets is just such a modification. Remember, if the glider was not certified with winglets, you are the test pilot. There is no guarantee that a spin will be recoverable.

A friend of mine has an ASW-20. He had been flying it for a number of years and was well acquainted with it, including its spinning characteristics. Then sometime after fitting it with winglets he encountered an inadvertent spin. Having plenty of altitude, why not leave it in for a while and see how it spins, he thought. To his amazement, when he went to recover it did not respond. Only by using the trick of pumping the stick back and forth, establishing a rhythmic oscillating pitch motion to momentarily get the nose down far enough to un-stall the wing did it finally recover.

REFERENCES:

First I want to thank Rick Lafford for all his advice and input. (6/4/03)

Material referred to: BGA Instructors' Manual; FAA Document AC 61 – 67B; Innovations in Stall/Spin Awareness Training, Rich Stowell; Spinning Machines, Tony Gee, Sailplane and Gliding Oct/Nov '94; Teaching Spinning, Chris Rollings (at the time BGA senior national coach), Sailplane and Gliding Jun/Jul '94; Teaching Spinning, Chris Rollings, follow-up to article of Jun/Jul '94, Sailplane and Gliding Oct/Nov '94; Spinning Modern Sailplanes, Howard Torode, Sailplane and Gliding Jun/Jul '94

APPENDIX 2

OFF-AIRPORT LANDINGS

An inordinate number of accidents occur during off-airport landings, which is regrettable as I am convinced the majority are attributable to pilot error and could readily be avoided by proper training.

Luck plays a surprisingly small role in successful field landings. Ninety-nine percent is know-how, preparation and skill.

I am reasonably qualified to address this subject having made, at this point in time, 169 off-airport landings and have probably picked ten times that number of fields. Consequently, most of the following material is based on personal experience including that in the "Must never do" category. Naturally, it is impossible for anyone to have been exposed to all possible scenarios, even in a lifetime of cross-country flying, so some of the material is derived from other pilots encounters.

Warning: There will be a test sometime after this course. The time and place will be at your first field landing and failing is not an option.

Kai Gertsen, April 1999 (Revised 2006)

WHY YOU SHOULD BE PREPARED

If you are a glider pilot, X-C or not, you should know how to safely perform a field landing.

Although you may not deliberately set-off cross-country, an off-airport landing is always a possibility when flying a sailplane. When flying locally, unless you always fly directly over the airport, there is the potential for misjudging the wind, or encountering excessive sink, thus finding yourself too low and too far away to get back to the airport. Selecting a field and landing safely, while there is still plenty of altitude to do so is much safer than attempting to stretch a glide to the airport with marginal height.

Even if you don't stray very far from home there is the chance of a rain or snow shower engulfing the airport, reducing visibility to below minimum. Selecting a field in the clear, rather than risking a landing in hazardous conditions at the airport is a much better option. Be especially vigilant of snow showers, they can be treacherous, reducing visibility to near zero in less than a minute.

Many years ago we were selling our KA-6. A fellow showed up and said he was interested, could he fly it? We didn't see why not and gave him a tow. Just then a snow squall moved in. He disappeared and did not return. This was somewhat disconcerting, this fellow whom we had never seen before had vanished with our glider. An hour or so later we got a phone call. He had taken the proper course of action and landed safely in a field, in the clear 9 miles away.

CONTEMPLATING CROSS-COUNTRY?

There are many pilots who deprive themselves of the joys of cross-country soaring because of their anxiety regarding off-airport landings. This is needless and regrettable. Cross-country flying is really what soaring is all about. Of course, it is possible to venture away from home with minimal risk of landing out other than at an airport by using the method of "Airport hopping". Nonetheless, serious cross-country flying cannot be done without the occasional visit with a farmer.

LEVEL OF RISK DURING A FIELD LANDING

Unquestionably, landing in a farmer's field does entail a higher level of risk than landing at an airport, but with proper preparation it can be done with an acceptable level of risk.

PREPARATION

It's not possible to practice all the situations we may encounter on our field landings, but we can envision a lot of the problems we may be faced with, and in our mind work out how we would deal with them. This is a very useful exercise and I strongly recommend it. Also, read all available material on the subject. Learning from other peoples experience is a lot less trouble than learning from your own.

Fortunately, some of the flying skills and judgment needed for safety in out-landings can be practiced right at your home base. Take full advantage of those opportunities — be prepared and stay safe. *(See page 123)*

SPIN PROFICIENCY

When the work load is at an unaccustomed high level, such as during an off-airport landing, that is the time you are most at risk of an inadvertent spin entry. You cannot afford to be ill prepared, recognition and correct control input must be intuitive. If you have to think about it, you will run out of time, recovery has to be intuitive.

Thorough spin training should be mandatory for all glider pilots, but to make the correct recovery procedure intuitive, spinning need to be practiced at regular intervals.

To be meaningful it is imperative that the training is done in a sailplane with similar spin characteristics as the sailplane you normally fly.

Spin training in a glider resistant to spinning, such as a Schweizer 2-33, is completely counterproductive as it will only serve to demonstrate that spins are nothing to worry about. Gross miss application of controls will only result in a halfhearted spin entry from which automatic recovery is instantaneous, regardless of control input. This sort of demonstration will lull the student into a state of complacency regarding spins, and leave him/her totally unprepared for the real thing. I do not know of any single-seat glider that will not enter a spin inadvertently, given the right conditions.

A significant portion of spin-ins occur during off-airport landings when a high work load diverts attention away from the task of flying the glider. No doubt many of those spin-ins are attributable to insufficient exposure to spins. Very few pilots recover from low level spins. So, practice, practice, practice — don't become another statistic.

THINKING AHEAD

Your mind must always be ahead of the sailplane, e.g. "If the present course is maintained and the present conditions (sink rate, ground speed, etc.,) persist, where will I be, one, two, and ten minutes from now?" Unless conditions are 100% reliable, be sure a safe place to land is within reach.

Always remember you fly a glider with your head, not your hands. Never let the glider take you somewhere your brain didn't get to five minutes earlier.

SERIOUS HAZARDS

Now that I have told you how safely this can be done, I'll highlight the hazards. Thought I would cover this while I have your attention.

The most dangerous hazards associated with off-airport landings are:

* WIRES
* SLOPES
* FENCES

Learn to cope with slopes, avoid wires and fences, and chances of ever causing serious damage to the glider or yourself are minimal.

WIRES

Wires are by far the greatest hazard, and the most often cause of serious field landing accidents. Every so often, there will be wires on the approach which cannot be seen in time to avoid them — wires, the invisible menace.

When we look at wires from the ground they appear quite visible. So, what are we talking about, "The invisible menace?" The problem is that when we are in the process of landing we are not viewing wires with the sky in the background, but against trees, earth, crop, etc. which tends to camouflage wires very nicely, and when the angle of light is unfavorable they do indeed become invisible. To assure we never make an unpleasant discovery, we must pretend there are wires where they are likely to be, and make the pattern and approach accordingly.

I have on several occasions skirted imaginary wires, and to my astonishment discovered them to be real — after landing.

There are likely to be wires:

* Between two poles.
* Between a pole and a group of trees, or a single tree. It is not uncommon to find a telephone pole hidden by one, or a cluster of trees.
* Between a road and a house.

125

- Above any road.
- Going to any kind of a building.
- A narrow field with trees on one side and wires along a road on the other side, or a field with trees along both sides may have wires crossing anywhere along its length. Avoid such fields if at all possible. The advice of landing well into the field is not applicable in these situations.

The safest assumption is to pretend there are wires around the entire perimeter of every field.

When crossing the boundary of a field pretend there is a wire there, then fly the approach high enough to provide plenty of clearance. It is not advisable to fly under a wire or wires as there could be a wire half way up the poles.

If you must make your final approach over high tension power lines, be sure to allow for the thin ground wire above the power cables, which may not be visible. This thin wire can be as much as 20 ft. above the power cables. Beware, the heavy- duty power cables will tend to focus your attention. The safest tactic is to make the approach above the height of the adjacent pylons.

The best way to minimize the potential for having an unpleasant encounter with wires, is to pick a field out in open country, away from roads, trees and buildings.

SLOPES

Obviously, the best way to deal with slopes is to avoid them.

In our part of the country (The Finger Lakes Region in New York State) we pick fields in the valleys as the terrain on the high ground tend to be hilly. Fields in the valleys, for the most part, are reasonably flat and level, they also tend to be bigger. Furthermore, when selecting a field in a valley you will have more altitude available in which to find a thermal.

As much as we try to avoid landing on a slope, there may come a time when there is no other choice. When flying directly above a field, slopes are undetectable. Fields should be viewed at an angle of 30° from the horizontal. When viewed from 30°, terrain features are considerably more evident. Flying directly above a field which you are contemplating landing in is a complete waste of time and altitude. In spite of viewing a field at an angle of 30°, any detectible slope will be steeper than you think, and too steep for a down-hill landing. You must land up-hill, regardless of wind direction.

Landing up-hill is tricky business, and as with so many other skills we talk about, one that we don't have much opportunity to practice. Yet, it is imperative that we get it right, and the only hope to get it right is to be well acquainted with the proper technique and the pitfalls.

Here are the fundamentals of an up-hill landing:

- During an up-hill landing it is crucial to pick up extra speed on final so as to be able to fly up-hill parallel to the ground, prior to flaring. The main objective is to avoid flaring into the hill, people have sustained serious injuries from doing this.
- The final should be started at the same place in the pattern as you normally do and at the same height (providing your normal height for starting the final leg is 300 ft.) then get the nose down to build up extra speed. What makes this maneuver even more challenging is that a strong illusion comes into play. When looking at an uphill slope on final, you will get a distinct impression that the glider is more nose-down than it is. Be sure to monitor the airspeed indicator.
- Go easy on the spoilers, chances are you may not need them at all. The speed will dissipate in a hurry once you start going up-hill.
- Do not use landing flaps, doing so will make the pull-up somewhat mushy which is precisely what you do not need.
- Landing uphill, into a stiff breeze is especially demanding, having the additional challenge of coping with heavy sink due to curl-over, wind gradient and turbulence.

Landing across a slope is not advisable. However, you could be faced with a situation where there is no other choice. If you must land at ninety degrees to a slope, keep in mind that the glider simply will not fly straight with one wing down. Landing from a conventional, straight-in approach will most certainly result in a vigorous ground loop and a broken glider. The only hope is to make the final in a turn to match the slope — easier said than done. The touch down must be on the upward portion of the slope so as to avoid rolling downhill.

FENCES

We are not so much concerned with wooden fences or fences with wooden posts, not that we want to run into them, but because they are quite obvious and should be readily avoidable. The type of fences we are concerned with are the single strand electric fences with thin steel posts, they can literally be invisible and deadly. Not that I want to over dramatize the subject, but some unfortunates have been decapitated. To avoid ever encountering this hazard:

- Never land or roll across two different crops.
- Never land or roll across the border of dissimilar textured surfaces.

A slightly different textured surface in one section of a field may indicate the presence of a fence. In many cases, such difference in texture is a result of grazing cattle having been confined to one section of a field by an electric fence – never cross such a boundary.

If you are approaching a fence or other obstacle on the rollout, and you realize that you are not going to be able to stop in time, the best course of action will be to ground-loop the glider. Remember to push the stick forward to lift the tail off the ground at the same time as you put one wing down, this will prevent the fuselage from breaking.

> *Life is simple. Eat, sleep, fly.*

WIND DIRECTION

Check wind direction periodically during any flight. Knowing in which direction you will want to land will be one less thing you need to sort out when you get down to the level where you need to look for fields. Here are some means of checking the wind direction:

- Drift when thermalling is a good indication of wind direction and strength.
- Smoke is the best indicator, but there are not as many smoke stacks as there used to be.
- Pond or lake surface. A wind shadow (calm area) will be next to the upwind shore.
- Drift of cloud shadows across the terrain. Keep in mind that there often is a difference between the wind direction at the surface and at altitude.
- When hunting on a ridge, hawks tend to hover directly into the wind, making an excellent weather vane.
- Waves in high crops, or grass.
- The wind in a narrow valley between two ridges will be parallel with the valley in spite of the wind direction being at 90° to the ridge at the crest.

FIELD SELECTION

- Do not rely on small private airports.

The width of a mowed runway of a small private strip is often only wide enough for a tricycle landing gear, but too narrow for a glider with a 50 ft wing span. If there are fully grown corn, or fences on both sides, you will be in big trouble.

There is a certain amount of risk in relying on a landable waypoint in your GPS, unless you are familiar with it. Supposing you are at about 1,500 ft, and it looks like you will be needing a place to land. You dial-up landable waypoints. Sure enough, there is one a mere 6 miles away. You arrive with 500 ft in hand. "Oh shucks! Too narrow. Now what?"

- A cut hay field is the optimum choice.
- Use visual judgment — not the altimeter.
- Be conscious of the terrain at all times.
- Look for a group of fields when down to 2,000 ft. Never rely on a single field in the midst of hostile terrain, always have some options.
- Retrieve convenience should never be considered when selecting a field. Always select the best and biggest field within reach regardless of convenience of roads, gates, restaurants, bars, etc.

1. There are enough prerequisites to be met when selecting a field, no need to add any more.
2. If the farmer can get his equipment into the field to cultivate it, you can get the sailplane out.
3. Never compromise your choice of field for the sake of an easy retrieve. Even a ten hour retrieve is insignificant compared with a damaged sailplane.

- If spotting a high-tension wire pylon, look for the others. You want to be sure you know where they are.
- At 1,500 ft, turn the radio off.

The radio will not help you to land or stay up, and those are the only two things that matter. Even listening to the radio is distracting. Getting low away from home is the most stressful situation you are likely to encounter in your soaring career, and the tasks at hand will require your undivided attention. *(See page 146)*

- A field must be selected by 1,200 ft.
- Once a field has been selected, do not change your mind.

Once a field has been selected, stick with it. This is not the time for indecision. On closer scrutiny you may discover some obstacles or troublesome features you did not notice earlier, but your best course of action is to make the best of it. Do what needs to be done to accommodate whatever difficulties you may be faced with. Trying to find an alternate field at this stage would be inviting disaster, this is not the time to change your mind. From 1,000 ft you only have about one minute until it is time to start the pattern.

- Once a field has been selected, you can consider it your base of operation and look for lift, but be sure you can reach the I.P. with comfortable altitude.
- On your first few off-field landings do not attempt to prolong the flight below 800 ft. Once you reach that level consider the flight over and concentrate on the field and making a safe landing. Thermalling low over unfamiliar territory, with minimal experience is definitely not advisable.

CROP & SURFACE

- A freshly mowed hay field (without haystacks) should be your first choice.
- Low crops may be O.K. Land parallel with the furrows between the plants. If you cannot see any ground between the plants, or you can see wind waving the crop, it is too high.
- High crops should be avoided, especially fully grown corn.
- If you must land in high crop, pretend the top of the crop to be ground level, and flare accordingly.
- Cultivated fields (raked) or freshly seeded fields will be soft, but the advantage is that all rocks and holes are readily visible.
- Plowed fields with deep furrows should be one of your last choices, in other words, when desperate.

However, should you have gotten yourself in a bind and wound up in an area where all the fields within reach are too small, a plowed field may save the day, as the roll-out will be extremely short. The question whether to extend the gear or not is debatable. One claim is that an extended gear offers more protection for the pilot. On the other hand, an extended gear may cause damage to the under carriage and will bring you to a stop very fast exposing the glider to high "G" loads.

- Use pastures only as a last resort.

Pastures are a poor choice, not only because they are probably not cultivated, but animals can be a real problem. Horses are unpredictable and may get excited. Cows are curious, difficult to keep away from the sailplane and likes to eat it. If you must leave the glider surrounded by cows, leave the radio on with the squelch turned off and the volume up, they don't like noise. If there is a single cow in a field, it's probably a bull.

FIELD SIZE

- As a rough idea, if there are no obstructions on the approach, 500 ft. may be adequate, but if you need to clear 70 ft. high trees, you will need about 1,000 ft. and if your speed control is less than perfect you may need more. But adequate size depends on a number of factors, such as:

1. Slope.
2. Wind direction and strength.
3. Obstructions.
4. Type of surface.
5. Type of sailplane.
6. Level of skill and experience.

- Another glider in a field may not necessary mean it's suitable for you.

It was a national contest and a lot of us were coming back to earth in the same area. A fellow competitor had landed ahead of me and invited me to join him, but I declined. The field had been more than adequate for his ASW-20 but there was no chance of me squeezing in there with my heavy Schueman Libelle, with its ineffective dive brakes.

- Your best bet is to pick the biggest, flattest field within reach.
- Visual illusions:

1. A narrow field will appear to be longer than it is.
2. A wide field will appear to be shorter than it is.
3. A long field will appear to be narrower than it is.
4. A short field will appear to be wider than it is.
5. If you have been low for a while, all fields will appear to be bigger than they are.

*   A longer field is needed if there is a lot of wind and turbulence.

When the wind is at 20 kts or more, you need plenty of speed throughout the pattern, right down to the round-out and hold-off. Consequently, you will need a little longer field than you normally would.

PATTERN AND APPROACH

*   A conventional pattern during any field landing is paramount.

Just because you are away from home, and the critical gaze of your fellow club members don't get the idea that you don't need to worry about a pattern. A proper pattern is more important during a field landing than at the home base.

If you ever make a straight-in approach to a field and it doesn't scare you half to death, you don't understand the problem.

This is not the time for the type of pattern we see from time to time, where the down-wind leg is much too close and too low such that the base leg is replaced by a 180 degree turn from the downwind leg onto final, and the final leg is virtually obliterated as that final turn is completed at a mere 50 ft — this is known as a 'button-hook' pattern.

It's a good idea to get in the habit of making proper, well defined patterns with the downwind leg adequately spaced to allow for a proper base leg and high enough to enable you to start the final leg at about 300 ft, positively no less than 200 ft. The pattern can be either right-hand or left-hand whatever is optimum, pending wind direction and terrain. If there is a crosswind component, make the base leg into the wind, if there are tall obstructions on one side fly the downwind leg on the other.

*   Do not start the downwind leg too high.

Some people have the idea that starting a little higher is better, but it isn't. If the correct altitude is 700 ft, then 1,000 ft is simply wrong. A correctly spaced, downwind leg is a critical element for a safe field landing. This is the only chance to scrutinize the field for rocks, holes, etc. so as to select a touch-down and roll-out area, and you'll be surprised how much detail you are going to miss from just a few hundred feet further away. Starting too high will also get you out of position for the rest of the pattern. Maintain proper distance during the down-wind leg so as to better evaluate the field and to leave plenty of room for a well defined base-leg.

- Don't rush the pattern.

Your first land-outs are likely to be a stressful experience and you may feel an urge to get it over with. Don't worry, the glider will come down in due time.

- Plan to land well into the field. *(For exception, see page 126)*
- If possible avoid making the approach over tall obstructions.
- If landing on a hill when the wind is 15 kts. or more, expect plenty of turbulence, and strong sink at the brow on the downwind side; do not extend the downwind-leg beyond the brow.
- Good speed control is imperative.

Do not confuse a low energy landing with a pattern flown at minimum airspeed. There is a lot of impetus on low energy landings. While it is true that modern gliders are slippery and we need to be extra careful concerning speed control, it is not advisable to fly the pattern at minimum speed. Always increase the speed in the pattern. You may be at the proper position and altitude, but if your airspeed is marginal the situation can deteriorate in a hurry should you encounter some heavy sink. With a little extra speed you are better prepared to cope with the unexpected.

The accidents which are caused by excessive airspeed are attributable to loss of speed control. To my knowledge no one has crashed because of approaching at an extra 5 or 10 kts. Be sure your speed is adequate to cope with the prevailing conditions, such as wind, turbulence and wind gradient. Select a speed that will make you feel comfortable and in full control. If it's an exceptionally short field, minimal speed may be necessary on the final leg.

- If too high on base leg use the 'Reverse Pattern Technique.'

If you should find yourself hopelessly too high as you are about to turn onto final, implementation of the 'Reverse Pattern Technique' will save the day.

Accidents due to overshoots are rare. Nevertheless, they do occur from time to time, which is a shame as they can easily be avoided. "Ah! This will never happen to me," you may say. It's not as unlikely as you think. Supposing, on one of your first cross-countries you are committed to a rather smallish field, you are surrounded by unfamiliar terrain and perhaps you have not been practicing landing without reference to the altimeter as often as you should have. Also, there is a tendency to be conservative and fly the pattern a little higher than normal during you first field landings and there you are — much too high. What to do?

The worse action you can take is to make a 360 degree turn, as it is difficult to predict the loss of altitude, and there is a real danger of becoming disoriented, especially in strange surroundings. Never lose sight of the field when in the pattern.

With the 'Reverse Pattern Technique' you can salvage the situation without stress or strain. You simply continue the base leg to the other side of the pattern while edging slightly further back so as to make room for a '180' which will lead you on to a perfectly normal base leg from the other side. During this entire maneuver you can apply spoilers as required while constantly keeping the landing site in full view.

If you are not familiar with this 'Reverse Pattern Technique' talk to an instructor, it may come in real handy someday.

- Landing diagonally across a field to increase the length of the landing area.

Providing the surface is suitable, if the field is short but wide, landing diagonally across the field will add considerable distance to the landing area. In a field 300 ft wide and 500 ft long, a diagonal approach and landing will add approximately 100 ft. Be sure to "clock" the pattern around to match the direction of the approach.

- Be flexible.

Although a standard pattern is important we must also be flexible. Supposing, while on the down-wind leg you notice the field has an undulating surface with 10 ft high crests, 50 to 100 ft apart diagonally aligned with the field. The prudent thing to do, irregardless of wind direction, will be to clock the pattern around such that you will be landing in line with and on top of one of the crests.

If you are short of altitude do not insist on a full pattern. In those situations the prime objective becomes to plan your flight such that the turn to final will be no less than 200 ft.

- Lower the gear.

If the sailplane is equipped with a retractable wheel, don't forget to lower it. This should be done at the same place in the pattern as you normally do, e.g. when entering the downwind leg. Then check it when on base.

WHEN TO OPT FOR A DOWNWIND LANDING

When the wind is light it may be advantageous to land downwind.

- As stated previously, if landing on a slope you must land uphill no matter what the wind direction is, whether the wind is minimal or otherwise.
- It may be better to land downwind with no obstructions on the approach than into the wind over tall obstructions.
- It may be a better choice to land downwind in a quality field than into the wind in a marginal one.
- If you are landing close to sunset do not land into the sun, regardless of wind direction, you will not see much of anything if you do. Fortunately, by that time there is seldom much wind.

On downwind landings there will be a significant increase in ground speed versus an into-the-wind approach, even in light winds. Prepare for a longer final by placing the base leg further back, so as not to get cramped.

LANDING

- Direction of landing.

The decision should be yours and yours alone. Another glider may have landed shortly before you got there, but don't let the direction in which that glider is pointed influence your decision making.

Years ago I made a field landing during a contest. The field wasn't the greatest and the landing resulted in a 180° ground loop. Another pilot arrived and did the same thing, so we were both sitting there facing in the opposite direction from which we had come. A third pilot prepared to join us. He assumed we had landed in the direction in which we were aimed and approached accordingly, going through some wires at the other end, ripping off the undercarriage. Of course, he blamed us for leading him astray.

- Be sure to stick with the touch-down and roll-out area you selected while on the downwind leg.
- Good speed control is imperative.

Be sure to maintain whatever airspeed you have determined to be optimum for the conditions, all the way to the round-out and flare.

- Always do a complete flare on every landing.

Since energy is proportional to velocity squared, even a small difference in speed at touch-down makes a significant difference in kinetic energy. Assuming a glider with a stalling speed of 40 kts landing at 45 kts. The extra 5 kts of speed would result in 26% additional energy to be dissipated upon contact with the ground. This number would go up to 56% if the glider was forced on the ground at 50kts.

If landing in high crop, be sure to flare completely above the top of the crop as if the top of the crop was the ground. If you are flying a sailplane with spoilers on the undersurface of the wing (fortunately, there are not too many of those left,) close the spoilers just as the glider is about to settle. If you do not retract them, inevitably the spoiler on one wing will contact the crop before the other, causing a vigorous ground loop. If you are flying a glider equipped with flaps, leave them in the zero position if possible.

• Once on the ground, apply full wheel brake.

Immediately after touch-down, apply the wheel brake to shorten the roll-out as much as possible. The longer distance you roll, the greater are the chances of encountering rocks and holes. Don't try to be clever and roll up to the gate for convenience, it won't look very clever if you roll in to a hole and wreck the landing gear.

• Forgot to lower the gear?

If you realize you forgot to lower the gear as you are about to flare — leave it alone. Attempting to extend the gear at that point in time can easily lead to pilot induced oscillations and a broken glider. It is next to impossible to cycle the gear with one hand and remain totally steady with the other, and any slight twitching of your "stick-hand" will result in P.I.O.s. Worse, if you didn't succeed in getting the gear down and locked you will be more susceptible to injury. On the other hand, a smooth and gentle landing on soft ground, with the gear up is likely to cause very little damage, if any.

QUALIFICATIONS

So when will you be ready to tackle off-airport landings? Aside from being thoroughly familiar with the content of this booklet you need to be comfortable with the glider you are flying. There are no set minimum hours, it is the number of flights that counts. If you recently have moved up to a new type of glider a good rule is, 10 flights before going cross-country. Another factor to take into consideration is the difference in flying characteristics between types. Once you

136

get into the higher performance gliders, the handling between types is very similar and the 10 flights rule may be overly conservative. The bottom line is, don't go cross-country until the task of flying and landing the glider is intuitive.

AFTER LANDING

- If you have landed at a private strip be sure to move the glider out of the way immediately so as not to block the runway.

During a Region III contest a competitor landed at a small private strip, abandoned his glider in the middle of the runway and left to make a phone call. The owner came back from a trip, was not able to land at his own airport and had to land someplace else.

This little airport is used extensively by the local glider pilots. We are very fortunate in having such places with friendly owners to resort to when the need arises, but let's not test their tolerance. We must be courteous and considered to the owners, or these oasis may not be available to us in the future.

If you are flying in a contest and have landed in a farmers field, there is a good possibility that if you can't stay up, there may be others with the same problem and you may get company. Before doing anything else, move the glider off to the side.

- Keep in mind that you *are* trespassing.
- If landing in a field with crop, next to a busy road, try to keep spectators out of the field as they can cause considerably more damage to the crop than your landing.
- Always contact the owner of the field if possible.
- If there may be a question of crop damage, take pictures of the landing path to defend any potential insurance claim.
- Be courteous, and respect the farmers property.

Ask the farmer for the best way of getting the sailplane out, and to get his permission before driving the car and trailer into the field. If you cannot locate the owner and there is crop in the field, do not drive in there, use some other means of getting the glider out.

I landed once on an Amish farm in Pennsylvania and I was puzzled over the cold reception I was getting from the otherwise friendly appearing farmer. Come to find out, a glider pilot had landed on his property some ten years before. that pilot had driven his trailer through a field of crop without bothering to ask permission. The memory of that pilot's crude behavior was quite vivid even after ten years. *I did finally manage to convince my host that all glider pilots do not necessary behave in the same manner.*

> *A superior pilot is one who stays out of trouble by using his superior judgment to avoid situations which might require the use of his superior skill.*
>
> **Arne J. Boye-Moeller**

- Prior to making the phone call, write down the directions to be sure they are complete and clear. Also, it is crucial to include the telephone number of the people you are with – enabling the crew to contact you in case they have any problems.

At first the farmer may very well view you as a rich city playboy (which may be entirely true) who has landed his expensive toy (also true) on his humble plot of land with complete disregard for other peoples property (hopefully, not true.) Here are some suggestion as to how you may conduct yourself to win him over:

- Be polite and courteous. Be sure to show appreciation for all his help including the use of his phone and don't forget to pay for the call.
- Impress upon him how fortunate you were that his field was there, enabling you to avoid a crash, and how happy you are not to have caused any damage.
- Emphasize how, in these rare emergencies, we always strive to avoid landing in any kind of crop.
- Show an interest in his farm. Ask questions and talk less about yourself.
- Take pictures of him, his family and kids next to, or in the glider.
- Don't forget to get his address so you can mail him copies of the pictures and perhaps a soaring calendar at Christmas to show your gratitude.
- Remember – you are an ambassador for the soaring movement.

The manner in which you conduct yourself will be a reflection on all glider pilots. A discourteous pilot will make a lasting impression on the locals, and future visiting glider pilots will be treated accordingly. You may have had a bad day but don't take it out on the farmer.

ELEMENTS OF A SUCCESSFUL FIELD LANDING

- RADIO OFF.
- EARLY DECISION TO LAND.
- VIEW FIELDS AT ABOUT A THIRTY DEGREE ANGLE.
- PICK THE BIGGEST AND FLATTEST FIELD.
- DISREGARD CONVENIENCE OF THE RETRIEVE.
- BE SURE SLOPE IS TOLERABLE AND LAND UP HILL.
- SUITABLE SURFACE, LOW OR NO CROP.
- TALL CROP, LAND ON TOP.
- ALLOW FOR WIRES AND FENCES.
- BE HEEDFUL OF THE AIRSPEED.
- AVOID LAST MINUTE INDECISION.
- WELL DEFINED PATTERN, RIGHT OR LEFT HAND.
- BE DISCIPLINED, YET FLEXIBLE.
- SELECT A SPECIFIC TOUCH-DOWN AND ROLL-OUT AREA.
- LAND WELL INTO THE FIELD.
- FULL FLARE.
- SHORT ROLL-OUT.

PRACTICE

Off-airport landings require many skills. Skills are acquired through practice. Fortunately, some of the skills essential to successful off-airport landings can be practiced without going cross-country. The more we practice, the better chance we have in getting it right when the time comes.

PRECISION PATTERNS

Get in a habit of making well defined patterns. Of course, that may not be possible on every flight. If you get back to the airport too low or encounter excessive sink in the pattern you must have the flexibility do whatever it takes to avoid making the last turn below 200 ft. Do not to start the pattern too high just because you got back with plenty of altitude. Get down to the correct altitude at the I. P. before starting the downwind-leg.

PATTERNS WITHOUT REFERENCE TO THE ALTIMETER

As frequently as possible enter and fly your patterns without reference to the altimeter. When it's time to come down, while still at 2,000 ft. or higher, tape a

139

piece of cardboard over the altimeter. This is a worth-while exercise as when the time comes for the real thing, the altimeter will be useless. This is in conformance with the FAA as you can lift the cardboard to take a peek anytime if need be.

LESSEN YOUR DEPENDENCE ON THE AIRSPEED INDICATOR

When the time comes to make an approach into a strange field there will be many other things requiring your attention.

PRECISION LANDINGS

Do not be satisfied with anything less than precision landings on every flight. Strive for perfection in speed control and spot-landing.

> *I would rather be in my glider*
> *And think about God,*
> *Than be in church and think about my glider.*
> **Arne J. Boye-Moeller**

FLARE COMPLETELY ON EVERY FLIGHT

Complete flare with minimum touch down speed must be practiced on every landing. When flying an SGS 2-33, do not get into the habit of pushing the stick forward, jamming the skid on the ground to stop. In a normal landing at the home airport, there is seldom any urgency to bring the glider to a stop, no great harm done by rolling another fifty feet or so. Habits are hard to break and can resurface without warning. This habit could sneak up on you during a stressful field landing in a high performance glider. Modern gliders do not respond well to that kind of treatment. Be sure you develop the right habits from the beginning.

To ease the construction of the flap actuating mechanism on my HP-14, I reversed the operation of the flap handle such that "forward" was "flaps down". This worked fine for the nine years I flew the '14' — no problem.

Then, years later I traded up to the Schueman Libelle with conventional flap operation. Being heavy, and with somewhat ineffective air brakes, field landings were challenging. Once I made a tense landing in a marginal field in S. C. On final, I was going like a bat out of Hell. What in the world?! Had the wind changed in the last minute? Getting out of the ship at the far end of the field I happen to glance at the flap handle. You guessed it, the flap handle was full forward, I had landed with full negative flaps — old habits never die.

PATTERNS WITHOUT REFERENCE TO GROUND FEATURES

Do not rely on terrain features such as barns, houses, etc. for establishing the pattern. Use only the landing area for reference.

Whenever the traffic allows, land at some other location on the airport. Doing a few of these before setting off into the unknown is well worth it. It gives you the opportunity to experience a pattern over terrain with different ground features than you are accustomed to. Remember, when landing out the *only* reference you will have is the spot where you plan to land. Another helpful experience is to fly at another site.

EVALUATING FIELDS

Don't let the drive to the airport go to waste. Although the vantage point is not quite right, it is still worthwhile to contemplate potential scenarios, e.g. which field would be better, how would you handle obstructions, consider various wind conditions, what would be the best approach, etc.

Practicing field selection can also be done while flying local. When down to 1,500 ft near the airport, pick a field. After landing, go over to the field and check it out. You will be surprised what it looks like up close. Such exercises are well worth the trouble.

The soaring site I operated at for many years has an eight hundred foot high ridge next to the airport, a perfect set-up for students to practice evaluating fields. You can pick a field on top of the ridge, fly part of the pattern, land at the airport, then drive up to the field to have a closer look. As you might have guessed, no one else bothered —too much trouble.

By practicing as many of the skills and simulating as many of the various hurdles which may be encountered when landing out as possible, we can significantly reduce the stress and work load when faced with the real thing. The objective is to have as few new challenges to cope with as possible on those first off-airport landings.

> *Glider pilots talk about yesterday, And dream about tomorrow.*
>
> **Helga Gertsen**

FLYING IN ANOTHER PART OF THE COUNTRY

When driving to another site you are not familiar with make it a point to look for features in the terrain which may be different from your home area such as, crops, slopes, fences, wires, etc.

On the way to a Region 6 North contest in Ionia, Michigan, known for its exceptionally friendly terrain, I made an interesting discovery. Whereas in other parts of the country, wires along roads are spaced at about 20 feet from the road, on many roads in the Ionia vicinity the poles are located several hundred feet into the fields. This is useful information to have beforehand. In case you are about to set-up for a landing with the approach over a road, better plan for the field being considerably shorter than it looks.

EMERGENCY PROCEDURES

- Landing in lakes.

If there are no fields in sight, lakes are preferable. Land parallel with the shore. Providing the canopy is either side or front hinged, unlatch it before landing, this prevents the canopy from jamming shut due to compression loads on the fuselage. Flaps should be set to the neutral position and the spoilers should be closed at touch-down. Flaps and spoilers were not designed for water loads.

Contrary to what may be intuitively obvious, it is important to lower the landing gear. It has been proven that there is less tendency for the glider to tuck under if the gear is down.

If a water landing is done correctly, the glider may well be flyable the next day. In some parts of Sweden water landings are done on a more or less regular basis as lakes are the only option other than trees.

- Landing in woods.
- If a landing in the woods is unavoidable, never pick a clearing with stumps. Select a large tree with a full crown. Set a normal pattern, be sure to approach the tree into wind, then stall, nose high into the crown.
- Collision avoidance.

If, with the sailplane on the ground and rolling, it becomes obvious that it cannot be stopped in time to avoid colliding with a fence, ditch or other obstacles – an intentional ground loop may be a better alternative. But delay it as long as possible. Be sure to move the stick forward at the same time when applying ailerons, lifting the tail to avoid breaking the fuselage.

Obviously we cannot practice any of these emergencies, but we can be mentally prepared. By envisioning any and all eventualities and pre-planning the optimum way of dealing with them, we can significantly increase our chances of keeping our skin intact if we should ever be faced with unpleasant options. The prime objective is to maintain control of the sailplane, not matter what the circumstances.

- Maintain Control

The important thing is to maintain control no matter how impossible a situation you may be faced with. You may not be able to save the glider but the chances of personal injury is highly unlikely.

> *I have known a great many troubles, but most of them never happened.*
>
> **Mark Twain**

HOW LOW IS TOO LOW

LOW SAVES

Many flights have come to a bad end because the pilot attempted to climb away from an impossible low altitude. Consequently, an in-depth discussion on the subject is prudent.

At contest, we are often enthralled by spellbinding accounts of heroic saves from 97 feet. However, it should be mentioned that some glider pilots have been known, on rare occasions, to stray ever so slightly from the perpendicular truth when relaying their aeronautical adventures. Also, there is an amazing illusion which mysteriously comes into play in these situations, which is this, 400 feet actually looks exactly like 97 feet.

In discussions on the subject of off-airport landings we often neglect to mention that the optimum course of action when faced with a field landing is, not to land; if there is a possibility to safely continue the flight, it makes sense to give it a try. Naturally, there will come a time when all efforts to continue the flight must be abandoned so as not to compromise a safe landing, and that's the big question, when must we commit to land?

Pundits are often asked, "How low is it safe to thermal?" This question hardly ever brings forth a definite response. Most often the question will be evaded entirely. The reason this question fails to bring forth a nice firm, quantitative answer which you can neatly tuck away and have handy when needed, is that there isn't one. The altitude at which the decision should be made to discontinue a flight depends on several factors such as, experience, level of skill, currency, familiarity with the sailplane, and weather conditions.

EXTRA AIRSPEED AND WELL-BANKED TURNS

Low level thermalling should always be performed using well-banked turns with an additional 5 to 10 kts of airspeed. One of the most often causes of stall and spin accidents are circling close to the ground in shallow-banked turns near stalling speed.

In a sailplane, it is far easier to stall and spin from a shallow turn than from a well banked one. In turns of more than 35 degrees of bank, due to the higher stalling speed, the control response remains firm and crisp until the last moment before the stall, and recovery can be made instantaneously without any loss of altitude by simply relaxing the backward pressure on the stick. In straight flight or a shallow-banked turn, the stalling speed is lower and control response get sluggish when approaching the stall. Should a stall occur, greater control input is required and recovery cannot be made without some loss of altitude.

The good news is that using well banked turns is no disadvantage as thermals at lower levels tend to be small, and steep turns are necessary in order to climb. Extra airspeed, also improves the climb as it enhances maneuverability which helps in dealing with low level, disorganized thermals. What's more, when making that first turn in what you think is a thermal and you are concerned about losing too much altitude if it doesn't work out, a 45° bank will get you around with minimal loss of height.

EXPERIENCE AND INSTRUMENTATION

One prerequisite which has to be met before attempting to thermal at low levels is that you must be capable of flying the sailplane with only occasional glances at the instrument panel as 99% of your attention has to be directed elsewhere. Consequently, any attempt to thermal will be severely impaired if your glider is not equipped with an audio variometer.

Although you may have acquired the level of proficiency outlined above, if you get down to 800 ft on any of your first few cross countries by all means abandon the flight and concentrate on the pattern and landing. Those first off-airport landings will tax your capabilities without further challenges. Do not attempt to thermal below 800 ft until you have a handful of field landings under your belt and begin to feel a little more comfortable in those situations. That is, sheer terror has been replaced by just a normal state of panic.

CURRENCY

You made good progress last year and reached new levels of performance; now it is spring and you are all primed to continue where you left off, but it has been six months since you flew last. Not being current is somewhat like being slightly intoxicated. You won't notice the effect till you get in a tight situation, as for example when trying to latch onto a couple of lumps of lift at minimum height over the boonies. So watch out, do not get too aggressive right-off, at the start of the season.

FAMILIARITY WITH THE SAILPLANE

Regardless of the level of experience you may have, if you are flying a type of glider which is unfamiliar to you it is a good idea to fly more conservatively until you get thoroughly acquainted with the glider.

SPIN PROFICIENCY

Inasmuch as we spend a lot of time flying near the stalling speed, proficiency in spin recognition, prevention and recovery should be a prerequisite for flying a glider under any circumstances. But definitely do not expose yourself to the additional stress and workload of low level thermalling over unfamiliar terrain until you have reached the level of spin training and practice which makes spin entry recognition and the correct control input for recovery intuitive. When the work load is high, as it is when trying to latch on to a feeble scrap of a thermal at pattern altitude while scrutinizing your selected field for obstacles at the same time, is when you are most likely to experience an inadvertent spin entry – better be ready.

To be fully effective, spin practice should be done in the glider to be flown, as spinning characteristics will vary from one glider to another.

If you have never spun a glider, be sure you get spin training in a two-seater with a qualified instructor prior to practicing on your own.

In order for this spin training to be of any value, it needs to be done in a glider that truly spins. Spin demonstration in a glider such as a Schweizer 2-33 is detrimental to spin training as it will inevitably leave anyone with the impression that it is virtually impossible to spin a glider, and recovery is instantaneous regardless of control input. Nothing could be further from the truth. I do not know of any single-seat glider that will not spin, given the right conditions. If you fly a glider long enough, sooner or later you will experience an inadvertent spin entry.

WEATHER CONDITIONS

In windy and turbulent conditions you need to raise the minimum altitude for attempting a save. There are days when it is not safe to thermal below 1,000 ft regardless of your experience level.

RADIO USAGE

Needless to say, the radio should have been off long before you get to this stage, if it isn't, by all means turn it off. Scratching around close to the ground, checking your selected field for slope, wires, fences and scrutinizing the intended touch-down area for stones, holes etc. while frantically attempting to center this scrap of a thermal you stumbled into at the last possible moment and, by the way, flying the glider at the same time, is most certainly the most demanding flying you will ever be faced with. Trust me, this will keep your mind fully occupied. The radio will not help you stay up, it will not help you land, and nothing else is of any consequence.

Incidentally, people have crashed because they were preoccupied with the radio. If you should fail to stay-up, any message to your crew can much better be transmitted at your leisure when you are safely on the ground. Besides, there is plenty of time, you won't be doing anything else that afternoon.

Even listening to a transmission is distracting. "KI, this is 1G, I am about 2 miles SW of Loon Lake at 8,000 ft, climbing at 7 knots." This may be interesting information for somebody, but to you, when struggling at 600 ft, it is totally useless. Worse than useless, because it can't help but divert some of your attention from the task at hand at a time when you can least afford it.

Hence, your best bet is to turn the radio off. My policy is to turn the radio off when I get down to 1,500 ft. I suggest you do likewise.

CRITERIA

The criteria I have used for many years is simply this, "If I can afford to lose 200 ft, I will try a turn. If I can't afford to lose 200 ft, I proceed with the pattern." Why 200 ft, you may ask. Well, on the average soaring day it is reasonable to expect areas of sink in the magnitude of 600 ft per minute. It is also reasonable to expect that you will turn in the wrong direction, which could place you very nicely in 600 ft per minute down. The rate of turn will probably be about 20 sec. per 360°. Consequently, you may be 200 ft lower by the time you complete the circle. If you expected this and planned for it, you won't get in trouble.

Let's assume you meet all the prerequisites. You have the experience outlined above, you are current and thoroughly familiar with the glider. You are on another cross- country flight. Things didn't go as expected, you are in the pattern to an apparent inevitable landing in an alfalfa field. You are half way along the downwind leg, and you feel a surge. Should you try a circle? If there will be enough height left to complete the pattern if you lose 200 ft, albeit, a little on the low side, but not uncomfortably so, you can give it a try. Hold off for a brief moment, if it feels solid roll into a 45° bank. With a little bit of luck, you may find yourself going up half way around so that you haven't lost or gained any height at the completion of the circle. Incidentally, this is about the best you can hope for on the first circle as the thermals tend to be small at that level. It is highly unlikely you will gain much during the first few circles. If you didn't lose any altitude, try another circle and if you can keep the variometer on zero, stay with it. The combination of your presence, helping to break the thermal free, and your centering efforts will in many cases eventually improve the climb rate.

However, if you continue to merely hold your own, you must be prepared to abandon the effort before you drift too far from the field. In case you eventually are forced to give it up, your effort will not have been completely futile as you gained some extra time to further scrutinize your selected field.

POSITION

Your position with respect to your chosen field is as much a consideration as your altitude. Crowding the pattern must be avoided. You should be in a comfortable position, off to the side. The distance to your selected field is all as important as your altitude, you may be high enough to circle, but if a 200 ft. loss will prevent you from reaching the entry point of the pattern at the appropriate height, don't try it.

If you do find yourself too low for a full, standard pattern, don't insist on it. The prime objective is to prevent the turn to final from being below 200 ft.

THE CLIMB

When starting to climb, you need to make a real effort to keep concentrating. There is a natural tendency to heave a sigh of relief and relax just a little when reaching a thousand feet, promptly losing concentration and the thermal.

A cease of climb at a 1,000 ft is not always caused by inattention. It is rare, but there are times when a thermal does not go any higher. Sometimes a thermal draws in excessive amounts of cold air and loses its buoyancy. A thermal may fade away when drifting in to the shade. At times like this, keep in mind that on any specific day, the thermals tend to sprout from the same source. Consequently, if you lose the lift before you get high enough to continue on course your best bet is to go back to the spot where you found it. Chances are there will be another bubble coming along which may have enough temperature differential to continue all the way up to the inversion.

ACCIDENTS

Most accidents occurring during attempts at low saves are attributable to:

- Distracted by the radio.
- Slow and shallow-banked turns.
- Work overload.
- Forgetting to fly the glider.
- Inadequate spin training.
- Not knowing when to quit.

> With grace and beauty, strength and cunning
> She'll stay aloft — until; inevitably — she loses
> And must glide earthward And lie there helpless
> Lovesick for the sky.
>
> **Leon Roskilly**

FUNDAMENTALS OF LOW SAVES

- BE SURE THE RADIO IS OFF.
- WHEN LOW, USE EXTRA AIRSPEED AND WELL-BANKED TURNS.
- AN AUDIO VARIOMETER IS A MUST.
- WHEN FACED WITH YOUR FIRST FIELD LANDINGS DO NOT ATTEMPT TO THERMAL BELOW 800 FT.
- STAY WITHIN YOUR CAPABILITIES.
- DON'T DO ANYTHING YOU ARE UNCOMFORTABLE WITH.
- NEVER THERMAL AT LOW LEVELS UNLESS YOU ARE EXPERIENCED AND CURRENT.
- NEED TO BE FAMILIAR WITH THE GLIDER.
- THE TASK OF FLYING THE GLIDER MUST BE INTUITIVE.
- MUST BE PROFICIENT AND CURRENT IN SPINS.
- RAISE YOUR MARGIN OF SAFETY ON WINDY AND TURBULENT DAYS.
- NEVER TRY A CIRCLE UNLESS YOU CAN AFFORD TO LOSE 200 FT.

- YOUR POSITION WITH RESPECT TO THE CHOSEN FIELD IS AS RELEVANT AS HEIGHT.
- DON'T FORGET TO FLY THE GLIDER.
- DON'T LOSE CONCENTRATION AFTER GAINING A FEW HUNDRED FEET.

> As I was flying through the air,
> I found some lift that wasn't there.
> It wasn't there again today — That's twice I've had to land away.

APPENDIX 3

INTRODUCTION TO CROSS-COUNTRY SOARING

This publication does not offer any new, brilliant strategies, nor does it reveal any deep guarded secrets. Most of the material presented here can be found in other publications, and have been used by glider pilots for many years. In fact, some of the techniques presented herein were used by pilots as far back as in the 1930s.

This is merely an effort to compile most of the practical aspects of cross-country soaring in one handy booklet for the aspiring cross-country pilot.

As the same techniques apply to contest flying, this material is also helpful for those intending to join the world of competitive soaring.

Kai Gertsen, April 1999 (Revised 2006)

INTRODUCTION TO CROSS-COUNTRY

As you read through this booklet you may get the impression that it applies to racing, and it does. However, though you may only be interested in recreational flying, you need to apply most of these techniques to some degree if you want to go somewhere. In bygone days when most of our flights were downwind dashes we didn't need to worry too much about efficient flying in order to get some sense of accomplishment. On most reasonable soaring days the wind usually blows at 15 mph, so if we managed to add a mere 25 mph we would cover a respectable 160 miles on a four hour flight, at 40 mph. Times have changed, 'Out and Returns' have now become fashionable. With that same performance, in similar conditions, it would take the same amount of time to complete an 'Out and Return' flight to a turn point 32 miles upwind.

In contest flying where every minute counts, you need to know and apply all of this material to the fullest extent.

TYPE OF GLIDER

While the latest ultra-performance glider with an L/D approaching infinity would be nice, an intermediate type with a glide angle of 30:1 will do well enough.

On the other hand, on the average eastern day, it is simply not possible to successfully practice many of the following cross-country techniques in anything with much less performance.

However, making your very first cross-country flights in a glider with a low wing-loading, such as a Schweizer 1-26 or K-8 is not such a bad idea as the low stalling speed and short landing characteristics will make those first off-airport landings considerably less stressful. When flying a glider with this level of performance the best policy is to stay as high as possible and don't pass up too many thermals. Also, chances are you will have more fun and less aggravation going straight downwind.

MAP PREPARATION

While navigation is done almost exclusively by GPS these days, it is a good idea to have a map available in case the GPS decides to close up shop. But to be useful, the map needs to be prepared for the occasion. Here is some helpful advice.

In a sailplane, we do not have the time or space to unfold and fold sectional charts. We need a single, one-sided map which covers the area we intend to operate within.

Unfortunately, the sectional charts have been carefully arranged such that most glider ports are located near the border of charts, so that typically two or more sectionals need to be joined together to create a one piece, single sided map. This can be done by using clear tape.

The next step is to draw five or six concentric circles centered around home base. The purpose of these circles is to enable you to readily estimate your distance from home when you are in the vicinity, and the altitude required to get there, basically turning the map into an oversimplified glide calculator. Space the circles at five miles increments. When working out the altitude required to get home, figure on losing 200 ft per mile or 1,000 ft per circle. These are nice handy, round numbers to work with and this gives you plenty of margin as it works out to an L/D of 26.4:1. Some allowance of course, has to be made for the effect of wind, which on most soaring days in the eastern part of the country amounts to about 15 mph. A good rule of thumb is to anticipate covering approximately 3½ miles per thousand feet, or losing 1,400ft. in 5 miles if going in to the wind. Downwind should get you about 6 miles for every 1,000 ft. loss of altitude.

In addition to the circles, mark all the turn points you intend to use in the future. If you operate within a contest area, mark your map with all the official turn points. When all done, it's a good idea to cover your map with clear vinyl to protect it from sweat and tears. The type made for covering kitchen cabinet shelves works well.

NAVIGATING BY MAP

Navigating by map need not be all that complicated; here is a simplified version. Before starting – with reference to the map and a prominent terrain feature such as a lake or town, point the glider on the heading you need on the first leg. Don't forget to make some allowance for crosswind. Note the compass reading, and now you know the compass heading for the first leg. Repeat this process after rounding each turn point.

If you are low and momentarily confused with respect to your position (in other words, lost), concentrate on getting as high as you can before trying to sort out your navigational problems.

GPS USAGE

If you will be using a GPS on your first cross-country, be sure you are well versed in its operation beforehand. By all means, do not try to figure out how to use a GPS during you first flight away from home, you will be busy enough as it is.

When navigating by GPS it is extremely useful to have an 8½" x 11" map with all the turn points, for quick reference.

OFF-AIRPORT LANDINGS

At some sites it may be possible to lay out a route which will permit airport hopping. Based on conditions in the eastern part of the country, the airport spacing should not be greater than 20 miles. The idea is that you don't go beyond reach of one airport until you are within reach of the next so as to avoid having to make an off- airport landing. This is an excellent way to get initiated and, if possible, the first few cross-countries should be done this way.

However, serious cross-country soaring cannot be done without an occasional visit with a farmer. Off-airport landings is a subject in itself and is covered in a separate publication. Field landings are not to be taken lightly, there is more to this subject than might be expected. On the other hand, don't let your apprehension of a potential field landing prevent you from pursuing the thrill and excitement of cross- country soaring. There is no question that off-airport landings entail a greater risk than landing at an airport, but if you are fully prepared, the risk can be contained to an acceptable level. Just be sure you are ready to cope with this challenge before setting off. Successful off-airport landings are 99% skill and 1% luck.

> Good judgment comes from experience, which comes from bad judgment.

THERMALLING

Efficient thermalling is a prerequisite for successful cross-country flying. In contest flying, it is absolutely imperative. On an average day, a couple of minutes more in each thermal can add 15 or 20 minutes to a 150 mile flight. That much time can be lost in the initial centering process alone if your performance is not up to par. Also, when thermals are feeble the right thermalling technique can make the difference between going up or going down.

Prior to solo flight, most training is concentrated on take-offs, patterns and airmanship, as it should be. Occasionally, when a thermal is encountered the student is instructed to circle, then to straighten out here and there. This is done mostly for the purpose of prolonging the flight. Some will receive some limited instruction in the basic principles of thermalling, but learning to center quickly and maximize the rate of climb needs special attention, and cannot be mastered before airmanship is fully developed.

Consequently, some pilots are a little short on thermalling technique, so it seems appropriate to cover this subject at the onset.

Some people believe going around in circles is all there is to thermalling. This is far from the case.

INSTRUMENTATION

A total energy compensated variometer is a necessity. Without it, any variation in airspeed will give false readings of lift distribution.

As we must be vigilant at all times for other traffic and at the same time monitor the variometer constantly, an audio variometer is also essential.

SKILL LEVEL

The prerequisite for being able to center thermals with a reasonable level of efficiency is the ability to make well-banked, coordinated, steady speed turns.

In addition to increasing the rate of sink, any slipping and skidding also changes the noise level, which is a major input we use in controlling airspeed.

It is absolutely essential to maintain a constant airspeed, as any variation in speed will skew the circle.

There is good reason to be proficient and comfortable at turning in either direction. When entering a thermal it generally pays to turn in the direction of the rising wing. When entering a thermal which is already occupied you have no choice, you must conform with the direction of turn already established. Accordingly, you will be greatly handicapped if you have a weak side. You may have a weak side and not be aware of it. If you use a data logger, check the flight statistics regarding one direction, you have a problem. The solution is to practice your weak side at every opportunity until you feel equally comfortable turning in either direction.

AIRSPEED

It is said that you should speed up in sink and slowdown in lift, which is all well and good but that does not apply in thermals. I have had the thrill of occupying the rear seat with a novice in the front who attempted to apply this technique while thermalling. The demonstration resembled a roller coaster ride and, of course, obliterated any sense of lift distribution.

The airspeed should be constant, and the optimum speed will depend on the type of glider and angle of bank. Some gliders climb better when flown near the stalling speed, in other types, performance improves if flown a little faster. It is imperative that you not be afraid of stalling the glider, if you have a fear of stalling you most certainly will tend to fly too fast.

If the thermal is broken up, or consists of a number of small cells, it may be advantageous to fly a little faster to maintain crisp, fast control respond to increase maneuverability.

ANGLE OF BANK

The most common mistake is not banking steep enough. Except when flying a glider with a very light wing loading, it is simply not possible to stay within the size of the thermals we typically have to cope with in the northeastern part of the country without using well-banked circles. Most often, if your angle of bank is not at least 35 degrees you are going to fall out of the thermal somewhere along the way. Keep in mind that 35 degrees of bank will seem like 45 degrees.

Thermals vary in size and structure from day to day, and the optimum rate of bank will vary accordingly. On a few occasions, if the thermal is fairly big, 35 degrees of bank might be optimum. If there is a strong gradient in the lift distribution, i.e. the lift is considerably stronger near the core, a steeper angle of bank works considerably better. Close to the ground, thermals are smaller and more broken up than they are at altitude. So if low, circle tightly at first, then as you gain altitude it may be advantageous to reduce the bank a little.

The ideal angle of bank will be somewhere between 35 and 60 degrees. A bank angle of 60 degrees generates a force of 2Gs, the stalling speed increases by 1.4 and the rate of sink increases correspondingly. Nevertheless, a couple of 60° turns in a strong surge can be well worthwhile.

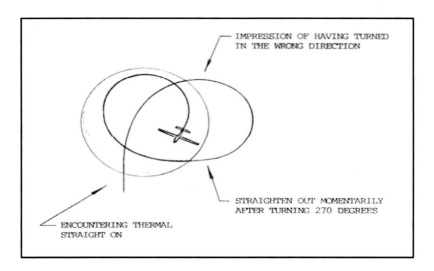

CENTERING AND OPTIMIZING THE CLIMB

The objective is to center as quickly as possible and maintain the optimum rate of climb until it's time to leave.

When looking for a thermal, the first indication that lift is near is an increase in the rate of sink. If you are heading in the right direction you are likely to encounter some turbulence as the rate of sink diminishes. Now get ready, and pay close attention to which wing wants to come up, as that will be the direction in which you will want to turn. This does not guarantee success, but it works more than 50% of the time.

In spite of having turned toward the rising wing you will, in all likelihood get the impression of having turned in the wrong direction. By the way, the chance of this happening is nine times out of ten. Don't get paranoid, this happens not only to you, this happens to everybody, and there is a logical explanation for this. In years past, when demonstrating thermalling techniques on a piece of paper, we indicated our flight path by drawing a circle tangential to a straight line. This, of course, is impossible. The path from the point where the turn is initiated to the point where the circle is established is not circular but elliptical. Thus, even though we turned in the right direction we may come out the side, creating the impression we went the wrong way. This is the reason it most often is necessary to straighten out completely after 270 degrees for a second or two. When back in the lift, immediately tighten the turn again. With a little bit of luck this should place you closer to the center. The objective is to form a mental picture of the lift distribution as soon as possible.

If the variometer shows some rate of climb all the way around, continue to shift your circle in small increments by reducing the angle of bank when lift is increasing, and then increase the angle of bank when the lift has peaked – timing is all important.

If the variometer actually shows sink on part of the circle you need to take a more drastic corrective action and straighten out completely to move the circle away from the sink. In this situation it's a common mistake not to straighten out completely, and not move over far enough, dreadfully going through the same sink twice. I think every glider pilot should have a plaque right across the instrument panel as a reminder, "I will never fly through the same sink twice."

Don't make the mistake of tightening the turn when you are in the sink in an effort to expedite the process of getting back into the lift, if you hold the turn on a bit too long it may have the effect of centering in the sink. Simply maintain the same angle of bank till it's time to straighten out.

Take time out occasionally for a glance skyward. There is a lot of information to be gained by observing the development of the cu you are circling under. It is especially beneficial to keep track of what's going on up above when beneath a small, thin, and short-lived cu. If the lift begins to taper off, intermittent checks will tell you if the cloud is dissipating, which is a good indication that it's not your centering that's gone wrong, but that it's time to move on. At other times you may notice another wisp forming next to the one you are under. This likely indicates another cell and since it is just reaching the condensation level chances are it is at its peak of development – better move over. Incidentally, there are usually two cells to a thermal. It also pays off to keep track of the more mature specimens. Bigger clouds are sometimes fed by numerous cells. The darker areas is where the cloud development is the deepest, and that is where the strongest lift is to be found. Be careful not to fall victim to "the grass is always greener" syndrome. "Is that dark patch over there really any better than the one I am under? Or would the one I am under look the same from over there?" – but that's what makes it interesting.

One mistake is to change direction of turn. In the rare instances when this maneuver is successful it is generally attributable to pure luck by accidentally stumbling into another core. As a means of centering, this strategy is totally useless.

If you lose the thermal entirely, you might consider making one shallow banked 360° circle, then tighten the turn if and when you re-enter. At times, it is tempting to prolong the search, but unless you are desperate it pays to move on after one circle.

When maneuvering within a thermal, control movements have to be timely but smooth and not excessive. Any control movement causes drag, which in turn increases the rate of sink. Be careful not to over-control. Look at it this way, if you are sharing a thermal with another pilot he should not be able to see any control movements.

Though you may have perfectly good instrumentation, don't ignore the sensations you get from your hindquarters. The first indication of entering lift will be an increase in, "G" loads, nose down pitch, noise level and airspeed. This feedback always precedes the response of the variometer.

Thermals are not the nice, well-defined, smooth columns of rising air that we like to depict them to be, but consist of a turbulent mass of bubbles and individual cores which are evident by surges of stronger lift. In addition to constantly shifting the circles toward the better side, you can further improve on the rate of climb by tightening the turn in these surges. A good strong surge is evident by an exceptionally pronounced boost from the seat pan. When you feel a surge, dig the wing in right there and hold a tight turn as long as the lift is solid. A strong core will have the tendency to push you out of it, when that happens tighten the turn even further, if possible. The instant the lift tapers off a little reduce the angle of bank ever so slightly, perhaps 10 degrees, but no more. This will cause a small shift, either bringing you back to center or bring you in contact with another core. Then tighten the turn again on the next surge. This may seem contradictory to the method outlined for centering, but think of this process as adjustments, rather than centering. Only maintain a steep angle of bank as long as the rate of climb is maximized. When hawks are thermalling they constantly make sharp turns here and there to take advantage of such surges.

Efficient thermalling is a combination of constantly shifting the circles toward the better part of the thermal and tightening the turn in the surges.

One key to maximizing the rate of climb is to never be satisfied. Achieving the ultimate rate of climb requires total concentration. I believe it was Justin Wills who said: "If you can make a radio transmission without some loss in the rate of climb, your rate of climb wasn't maximized to begin with". Centering is a never-ending process, you are not likely to experience a fixed rate of climb all the way around for very long. Whenever the rate of climb is slightly different on part of the circle you need to take action, it won't improve on its own.

In the interest of safety, when sharing a thermal with other gliders, do not make any erratic moves, the other pilots should be able to anticipate your intentions. For example, changing direction of turn just as another glider approaches, intending to join your thermal, could possibly put you at risk of a mid-air. When in a sizable gaggle you will not be able to implement all of the tactics proposed in this section. If you did, you most certainly would be most unpopular. When joining a congested thermal, you don't have much choice but to jump on the carousel, pick a slot and follow the crowd. You simply will have to settle for a slower rate of climb. But that's the price you pay for the security of staying with a gaggle.

WHEN LOW

For safety reasons, low level thermalling should always be performed using well banked, coordinated turns with an additional 5 to 10 kts of airspeed.

Many stall and spin accidents are caused by circling close to the ground in gently banked turns near the stalling speed. In a sailplane, it is far easier to stall and spin from a gentle turn than from a well banked one. In level flight or shallow- banked turns, the stalling speed is lower and control response gets sluggish when approaching the stall. Should a stall occur, greater control input is required, and recovery cannot be made without a significant loss of altitude. In turns of more than 35 degrees of bank, due to the higher stalling speed the control response remains firm and crisp until the last moment before the stall, and recovery can be made instantaneously without any loss of altitude by simply relaxing the backward pressure on the stick.

The good news is that using well-banked turns and a little extra speed is no disadvantage as at lower levels thermals tend to be small and broken. Steep turns and more speed for increased maneuverability are necessary in order to climb well.

OTHER METHODS

After all is said and done, thermalling is more of an art than a science. I can only recommend what works for me, but many top pilots advocate techniques which, in some cases are not only different, but entirely contradictory to my approach. Indeed, it is difficult to find two books on the subject of soaring which are in agreement with one another on the subject of thermalling.

Here is a sampling of recommendations from other publications, written by some of the best: Instead of straightening after 270 degrees, change direction of turn; wait 5 seconds before turning; tighten the turn in sink; straighten out in a surge, then change direction of turn. These various techniques obviously work for the authors. From this, you may think anything works, but that's not the case. On a few occasions I have watched in amazement from the rear seat, as a student (apparently having read the wrong book) consistently shifted the circles out of every thermal.

There are, and have been a few world champions who do not even believe in tight turns, they merrily go around in 25 degree banked turns; out-climbing everyone else – seems like pure magic to me.

Ultimately, you will settle on a style which works for you, possibly consisting of a combination of different methods. Occasionally getting out-climbed is an indication that a change in your method may be in order.

CENTERING BY USING LIFT GRADIENTS

There is another method of centering which utilizes gradients of lift to seek out the position of the core by the amount of tilt these lift gradients impose on the glider. This method is based on the cross-section of thermals being roughly circular and consisting of lift gradients centered around a core, with the strongest lift at the core and gradually diminishing toward the perimeter. Here is how this works:

1. If the lift is minimal and the tilt is pronounced, you are near the perimeter with the core at about 90 degrees. Make a medium turn toward the rising wing.
2. If the lift and tilt is moderate, you are somewhere between the core and the perimeter. Turn more aggressively toward the rising wing.
3. If the lift is strong and there is no tendency for either wing to come up, your course is straight for the center. Weave slightly to one side and then turn sharply in the other direction.

Due to the size of thermals and the airspeed which we approach them at, to use this method you must rely on your physical sensations, as your reactions would be far too slow if using the variometer.

Yet there is a world record holder who doesn't even believe in turning toward the rising wing, claiming that tilt is totally random.

ELEMENTS OF THERMALLING

*   Timing is all important.
*   Always turn toward the rising wing.
*   When encountering a thermal low do not hesitate, turn immediately.
*   If you have enough altitude don't turn until the climb rate approaches your expectations.
*   When you do decide to turn, bank steeply right away, 35 degrees minimum. If you get the impression of having turned in the wrong direction, straighten out momentarily after 270 degrees.
*   Establish a mental picture regarding lift distribution.
*   Do not change direction of turn.

- Shift aggressively if there is sink on one side. Never go through the same sink twice.
- If there is some lift all around, shift in small increments.
- When lift is increasing, reduce the bank to move the circle in that direction, in small increments.
- Do not over-control. Control movements must be timely but no more than needed.
- Take advantage of surges. Tighten the turn on the surge, and decrease the angle of bank slightly when the lift drops off. Then tighten the turn again on the next surge.
- If you lose the thermal, make one wide 360°, then tighten the turn when you re-enter. Limit the seach to one 360°.
- Steeper turns are needed and safer when low.
- If you are low, do not leave what you have for something better.
- When sharing a thermal with other gliders, do not make any erratic moves, and keep track of everybody.
- Concentrate and never be satisfied.

RACING PILOTS HATE ALL THERMALS, AND SPEND AS LITTLE AS POSSIBLE TIME IN THEM

Once you have mastered the art of thermalling there are really only four things you need to know to successfully go cross-country, which are:

1. HOW TO FIND THERMALS
2. WHERE TO GO
3. HOW FAST
4. WHEN TO THERMAL

HOW TO FIND THERMALS

As with anything else in the art of soaring, when it comes to finding thermals nothing is for certain. But unquestionably, if you know and seek out the places and conditions where thermals are likely to be found, your rate of success will be significantly better than if you simply rely on running into thermals by chance.

Undoubtedly, there will be times when you simply happen to stumble into a perfectly good thermal when you least expect it.

FINDING THE FIRST THERMAL

A ground launch takes you to a fixed release point every time and, unless there happens to be a thermal right there, you will need to go look for one. An aero tow takes you to a thermal. That is the prime advantage of an aero tow over a ground launch (winch or auto tow,) not necessarily the additional altitude.

The advantage of releasing in a thermal is obvious, especially in a low performance glider. In a low performance trainer you will have more time searching for a thermal while on tow than after release. Many pilots have become programmed to tow to 2000 ft on every flight, and would never think of doing anything different. They will get dragged through perfectly good thermals but insist on getting their money's worth and stay on tow till they reach 2000 ft. By this time they are generally in sink, and will frequently be on the ground in record time. Even in a high performance sailplane, it is advantageous to get off in a thermal at a thousand feet rather than hanging on. Releasing before you reach the conventional tow height also gives you more practice at thermalling.

So how do we go about releasing in a thermal? The first step is to get in the right mind set. Change your objective; instead of towing to a fixed predetermined altitude, tow to a thermal. The timing is crucial so it is important to be mentally prepared. Decide beforehand the minimum altitude at which you are prepared to release at. This could be a thousand feet, or whatever you feel comfortable with.

Once you have reached your prescribed minimum altitude and the tow plane enters a thermal, evident by a sharp increase in climb rate, watch the tow plane closely, if it hasn't flown through the thermal by the time you reach the edge of it, release right then and there.

The timing is critical, this is the reason it's important to have predetermined the altitude you are willing to release at, there is no time to think about it, a couple of seconds hesitation can make the difference between success and failure.

Immediately upon release make a well banked 360° circle to the right and then proceed to center the lift.

It is crucial to maintain a steady tow position, so when the tow plane rises above the horizon it really is the tow plane going up and not the glider going down.

Keep tab on the rate of climb during the tow. Entering 'normal air' after having gone through a prolonged stretch of sink, the tow plane's rate of climb will increase. If you had not been keeping track of the climb rate, this could lead you to believe a thermal is at hand.

It is normal to be somewhat reluctant at first to release at a lower altitude than you are accustomed to, but keep working on it. Once you get the hang of it, you will need fewer relights, get more satisfaction and more thermalling practice.

DETERMINE THE RELATIONSHIP OF LIFT TO CLOUDS

Exploring the conditions before pushing off is a good idea. A half hour can be well spent in establishing where the lift is with respect to the clouds. It is not always upwind or on the sunny side, but whatever the relationship is, it will tend to hold true for the rest of the day. This bit of knowledge should minimize the amount of searching and fumbling associated with getting established in each thermal.

The leaning of thermals due to wind is more pronounced at lower levels, and becomes more vertical as the thermal approaches cloudbase.

SPACING OF THERMALS

Spacing of thermals is proportional to the height of the convection layer. There are few things in gliding which are for certain, but this is one of them. When the convection layer is shallow the thermals will be closely spaced. This is the reason cross-country flights are possible on days with low bases. Conversely, expect a long way between thermals when cloud base is high. Therefore, if you find yourself at 2000 ft. on a day when the thermals go to 8000 ft., you may be in trouble.

STRENGTH OF THERMALS

There is a rule of thumb relationship between the depth of the convection layer and the strength of thermals. For example, if cloud base is 4,000 ft you can expect to find a couple of 4kt thermals, the rest will be roughly two-thirds of that. If the base is at 6,000 ft a few thermals will be 6 kts, the rest 4 kts. When the lift goes to 8,000 ft....and so on.

EVALUATING CLOUDS

A sharp, well defined base and a cauliflower, crisp outlined top is what you should be looking for. A large cu is likely to be fed by several cells, the darkest part of the base is an indication of the deepest vertical development, and that is where you are likely to find the strongest lift. A sure sign of strong lift is a domed shape base. A ragged base with a broken, crumbling top is a sure sign of decay.

As I am sure you already have discovered, on a day with cu all clouds do not have a thermal. On a good day, about one cloud in three works well. When the air is dry a greater percentage of cu will be active. On a day with high humidity, only about one in four or five will have a thermal feeding it. Amazingly, there are also days when there does not seem to be any connection whatsoever between thermals and clouds.

Do not confuse long vertical tendrils of vapor with a ragged cloudbase. Tendrils are signs of exceptionally strong lift. These tendrils are mostly found when flying along the border of two air masses with different moisture contents.

When the sun is low, as at noon in mid-October, the clouds will appear to be better defined when looking toward the sun than they do when looking away from the sun.

When low, evaluating the terrain for likely trigger spots as you do on blue days will be more helpful than cloud reading. It's difficult to judge the degree by which a column of rising air is leaning. Also, a cloud may be as good as it looks, but the lower portion of the thermal has expired, and your search will be futile. This is especially the case on windy days when the thermals get sheared off from their source or trigger point and rise as isolated bubbles.

Just as there are clouds with no thermal attached, there are thermals which have not yet formed a cloud. If, while heading for an attractive cu, you stumble upon a good thermal out in the blue, by all means take it.

FOLLOW TERRAIN FEATURES ON BLUE DAYS

Don't be discouraged by the absence of clouds. Paul Bikle once remarked that the advantage of blue days is that you don't waste a lot of time chasing after dead cu.

Reading the terrain not only applies to blue days. If you get low you will do better reading the terrain than the clouds. It is difficult to predict how much a thermal is leaning. Also, the thermal feeding the cu you are aiming for may have left the ground long time ago.

You can expect thermals at the higher levels of upward sloping terrain facing the wind. As the air from the lower levels moves up the slope to higher elevations with cooler surrounding air, it becomes unstable. Such areas tend to be fertile ground for thermals.

At times, thermals stop just short of reaching the condensation level, but get close enough to form haze domes. These haze domes are excellent markers; always look for those on blue days.

A long ridge with the terrain sloping up on both sides to a crest can be used to great advantage, even in light winds, or when the wind is parallel with the ridge. On most days there will be thermals along such a spine, often spaced close enough to permit straight cruising.

WINDY DAYS

On windy days, a warm air bubble over a heat source gets displaced by the wind before it has a chance to gain enough buoyancy to break away. It will drift with the wind, gathering more warm air as it moves over the terrain until it reaches a triggering feature which can be just about any discontinuity in the terrain such as a line of trees.

On such days look for features in the terrain that might trigger thermals such as rivers, border of woods, and end of ridges. The cold air over small lakes can often trigger thermals. The dome of cold air above the water makes an excellent trigger for thermals as they drift with the wind across the terrain. This is especially the case in early summer when the temperature differential is significant. On the diagram on page 20, envision the wind being at ninety degrees to the lake and you have a classic example. This is the reason we often find ourselves thermalling over small lakes. Of course, the thermal is not generated by the lake, but is triggered by the shore and leaning out over the lake.

ON DAYS WITH MODERATE WINDS

When the wind is not too strong the domes of warm air are able to remain in place to attain buoyancy and rise up directly from the heat source. The thermals will be either columns of rising air or a series of closely spaced bubbles. This is when you will want to go for the hot spots like, ridges facing the sun, dark patches, gravel pits, towns and ripe wheat fields – wherever you wouldn't want to be walking around on a hot day.

A bubble over a field which hasn't quiet reached the buoyancy needed to break free on its own can be released by a tractor driving across the field. It is even possible for you to trigger your own thermal by flying through such a bubble. Well over 50% of the time when launching by car or winch, there will be a thermal right at the top of the launch. This is not likely to be coincidental. No doubt the thermal is triggered by the cable/rope, and glider cutting through a bubble, thus releasing it from the boundary layer.

At the beginning I mentioned that some of the techniques described here have been used for many years. Here is an extract from *The National Geographic Magazine, ca. 1936:*

> A modern sailplane flight in competition is never over until the ship is actually on the ground, and stubborn pilots, fighting to the last for a breath of breeze that would keep them in the air, discovered something.
>
> They found that if a man dived his ship at high speed, 70mph or so, above a promising source of a thermal current such as a corn field, banked sharply when only 1-200ft from the ground, and spiral upward in tight climbing turns, a surprising thing sometimes happened. A sudden thermal current caught the ship and carried it up, up, up, to the neighborhood of the clouds again. The swirling sweep of the 50ft wingspread, traveling at 70mph and suddenly twisting upward in a corkscrew fashion, had apparently dislodged a thermal bubble which had been on the verge of rising.
>
> When the first report of this came from a pilot in Germany, most American soarers were sceptical. But they tried it and found it often worked. Meteorologists say it is entirely credible.

(I suspect this article was embellished somewhat, but the basic concept is there.)

BIRDS AND OTHER SAILPLANES

A soaring bird circling, or a swarm of swallows chasing insects caught in a thermal is a good indication of a worthwhile thermal. A circling sailplane may not be. There are some pilots who never met a thermal they didn't like, and will go around in just about anything. Avoid needless detours, before joining another sailplane, be certain that it is indeed climbing at a worthwhile rate. If it is, don't hesitate, move over right away.

If you encounter another cell before you reach another glider in a thermal it pays to make a turn in case the one you stumbled into is better. That is the best chance you have to gain on the glider above you.

You can generally be assured to find lift when entering a thermal above another glider. Entering below another glider is another matter. There are times when the other glider is in a bubble and you happen to be bellow it, your rate of sink continues as the other glider climbs away. That sort of thing can get on your nerves.

OTHER GLIDER AS A THERMAL PROBE

Sharing a thermal with another glider is like having a remote thermal probe to indicate where the best air is. It works better than any variometer. By closely watching the vertical displacement of the other glider around the circle you will get a perfect picture of the lift distribution. But for this to work you must be at the same altitude.

SMELLING THERMALS

There has been some claims made that thermals can be located by smell. While it is true that smells do get carried aloft by thermals it has been my experience that by the time my nose picks up the scent the variometer is already telling me what I need to know. Your nose won't lead you to a thermal.

Be careful, the aromas drifting skyward do not all derive from freshly baked bread or sizzling bacon. Some fertilizers are potent. Once I encountered a thermal coming off a fertilized field. It didn't take long before my eyes started burning, it got so bad it was almost impossible to keep them open. It took quite some time before my condition improved. I was thankful a landing was not imminent or I would have been in serious trouble.

APPROACH THERMAL SOURCES IN LINE WITH THE WIND

The possibility of intercepting a thermal if approaching a potential source at ninety degrees to the wind is not very good as it is difficult to estimate how much a thermal is leaning, especially on days when the wind is rather brisk. The chances of connecting are much better if you approach the thermal in line with the wind. The same technique applies when attempting to connect with a cloud, when some distance below it.

EARLY EVENING SOURCES

These days we seldom use the entire soaring day. In competitions we race around for a couple or three of the best hours of the day. When flying for pleasure, most like to be home for cocktail hour. Nonetheless, in the unlikely event you should get caught out as the sun gets low, here are a couple of prospects to keep in mind.

Wooded sections, having soaked up heat throughout the day will be releasing it as the surrounding terrain cools down. These evening thermals only seem to be workable at some reasonable altitude – stay high when the end of day approaches.

In hilly country, as evening comes on, and the wind is light or non-existing, the air on the high ground cools and slides down the hills into the valleys (Katabatic Wind), forcing the air in the valleys to rise. This kind of lift is as smooth as wave lift.

FLYING A GLIDER IS THE NEAREST YOU CAN GET TO HEAVEN. (WITH YOUR CLOTHES ON)

Hans Christensen

Kai Gertsen

WHERE TO GO

RESIST TEMPTATION TO TURN BACK

In the event you encounter a prolonged stretch of sink immediately after heading out on your first few cross-country attempts, you may be tempted to make a 180° and go back home. This is generally a mistake as you will then be flying through the same area of sink you just went through on the way out, and may find yourself with marginal altitude to reach the airport.

IF ENCOUNTERING A LONG STRETCH OF SINK, TURN 90°

If you are in sink and it persists, chances are that you are on a street, unfortunately the wrong kind. Your best bet in this situation is to change course by 90°. Stay on that heading until the sink subsides, then get back on course.

CYCLING

Generally, the cycle time for thermals on an average soaring day, in the eastern part of the country is 20 minutes or so. As heat is in short supply in the beginning of the day, the first cu only last for a few minutes. As the day matures the cycle times get longer.

Although small wisps of cu's with a lifetime of a few minutes mostly occur during the early hours of a soaring day, there are times when that's all we get throughout the day. Even though you may not be able to reach them before they evaporate, it can be worthwhile heading their way as they will probably recycle, and the time between cycles are short.

Keep in mind that thermals tend to trigger from the same source throughout any given day.

HIGHER TERRAIN

In hilly or mountainous regions stay over the higher terrain. That is where small wisps of cu will first appear and where the soaring conditions will be notably better throughout the day.

WATCH CONDITIONS A-HEAD WHILE CIRCLING

You should know where to go before reaching the top of your climb. Since we need to limit the number of thermals we use, try to select the next climb some

171

distance out, ideally with some cu along the way that you can string together. Be on guard against selecting a good looking cu which may have reached its peak of development, and may be all spent by the time you get there. To prevent falling into this trap you need to have some idea of the cycle time, how long the cu has been there and how long it will take to reach it. A better bet may be to choose a cu in the early stage of growth. If you see a promising wisp, check on it every 360°, this will give the effect of time lapse photography, revealing whether it's developing or dissipating. Have a backup or two in case your first choice doesn't work out. As in chess, always think two or three moves ahead.

JUDGING DISTANCE TO CLOUDS

Judging the distance to the next cloud can best be done by looking at the cloud's shadow on the ground. It is virtually impossible to get any sense of distance by looking directly at a cloud. Also, when close to cloudbase, the best indication as to how the cu's line up and the direction of cloud streets is to look at the shadows.

FOLLOW PATHS OF LIFT

Following paths of lift will significantly improve performance in spite of such detours not always deliver what they promise. Supposing you go out of your way to follow some scattered wisps resulting in a zigzag course of 15°, and the result was disappointing, only reducing the sink rate by half. Nonetheless, it was well worthwhile. Think of it this way, your glide ratio got doubled, and the extra distance flown over a 20 mile stretch would only be three-quarters of a mile. Even greater detours do not add as much distance as you may think.

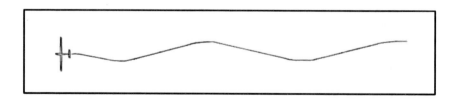

DEGREES OF ZIGZAG COURSE	INCREASE IN DISTANCE OVER 20 MILES	
20	1.2	"
25	2.0	"
30	3.0	"

STAY UP-WIND OF THE COURSE LINE

On a windy day, strive to stay upwind of the course line at all times. Heading down-wind should only be done in desperate situations, e.g. to remain airborne. Of course, this becomes less significant on days with light winds. But on a day when the wind is 20 knots, getting back on course after a slow climb originating downwind can be difficult, exasperating and time consuming, but may not even be desirable. If you have drifted significantly off-course the prudent thing to do is to draw a new course line (your GPS will do it automatically) from your position to the goal and abandon the original. Remember, your compass heading will now be different. Beware, you may experience an inherent urge to get back on the original track.

FOLLOW CLOUD STREETS

It usually pays to follow streets even if they are as much as 30° off track. Cross over to the next street at 90° so as to spend the least amount of time in the sinking air between the streets. The rate of sink between well-developed streets is likely to be much greater than what we normally encounter between cu.

When flying beneath a street, going downwind, don't expect the last cu in the street to be of much help.

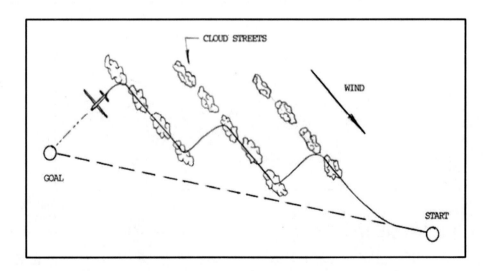

UTILIZING CLOUD STREETS 90° OFF-COURSE

Occasionally a cloud street as much as 90° to the intended track can be helpful. You are about to cross a sizable hole, and the crossing looks marginal because of a strong cross wind. Supposing there is a good, solid looking street going upwind at the edge of the hole. If it is good enough to enable straight cruising at cloud base, it can be worthwhile to follow it upwind for a few miles. You can then set off across the blue with a quartering tail wind with a much better chance of reaching the other side.

This technique also comes in handy when on a ridge running mission, and the thermals don't go high enough to get you across a gap. If the wind is blowing hard enough to make the ridge work, the thermals are likely to be streeting. So when topping off a thermal just short of the gap, fly directly into the wind. With a little bit of luck you will be able to utilize a line of thermals to penetrate far enough up wind to get across.

LINE UP WITH STREETS BEFORE YOU REACH THEM

If there is a cloud street ahead, the likelihood of flying in better air is increased if you line up with the street long before you actually reach the clouds.

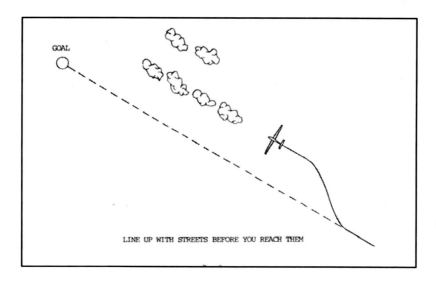

GOAL

LINE UP WITH STREETS BEFORE YOU REACH THEM

FORMATION OF STREETS

Thermals will tend to organize into streets whenever the wind velocity is 12 kts or more, and there is no radical change in wind direction up through the convection layer. The streets are commonly spaced at roughly three times the depth of the convection layer. Also, it helps considerably if the sun is at 90 degrees to the wind. The cloud shadows between the streets will reinforce the

174

streets by blocking thermal formation between them. If the sun is in line with the wind the cloud shadows will fall directly below the street hampering its development. In fact, this may prevent formation of streets altogether.

On most days, if there is any wind at all some form of streeting will take place, although there may be no visible evidence. Hence, the next thermal is probably closer either upwind or downwind.

STREETS ON BLUE DAYS

As is the case on days with cu, if the wind is 12 kts or more, and there is no significant change in wind direction up through the convection layer, the thermals are likely to form in streets aligned with the wind, notwithstanding the absence of clouds. Streets on blue days will not be as well defined as they are on days with cumulus clouds, as they are not being reinforced by cloud shadows.

RIDGES AS LAST MINUTE SAVES

A ridge can often be used to prevent a premature landing. If there are ridges in your area, always plan ahead so that you can reach a workable ridge if all else fails. Preferably one with a suitable field at the base. Then you simply stay on the ridge until a thermal comes by.

When hunting on a ridge, hawks tend to hover directly into the wind. Making an excellent weather vane. A good indicator of the angle of the wind to the ridge.

A thermal will ruffle the tree tops in a rotary motion as it drifts across a ridge. When ridge soaring, waiting for a thermal, this kind of vortex in the tree tops is a helpful sign.

Thermals are often triggered at gaps and at the end of ridges. A funnel shaped upward sloping ravine, perpendicular to a ridge facing the wind, is almost certain to produce thermals.

When getting a thermal off a ridge, and the combination of wind and rate of climb is such that you are drifting down wind faster than you are climbing, making it difficult to get away, look for the next thermal well upwind of the ridge. If the wind is strong enough to make the ridges work, the thermals will probably be streeting. Head directly into the wind from the thermal you just left. Go as far out from the ridge as you feel comfortable with before taking a thermal, and you will have a much better chance of being able to stay with it and get on your way.

PLACES TO AVOID

WET TERRAIN

It pays to avoid wet terrain. It's helpful to have some idea where it rained, or what areas had the heaviest rainfall the night before. If it's not possible to avoid such areas, proceed with caution.

River-valleys are usually troublesome, avoid them if possible. If you must cross a river-valley, expect soft conditions.

Again, nothing is for certain. In the month of March half of Florida is submerged, yet, the soaring conditions are often quite good.

DOWN-WIND OF LAKES

Given the right conditions, even small lakes can generate clamps. If the lake is elongated, 10 miles or more in length, and the wind direction is along the lake, you may find a significant area of stable air down-wind.

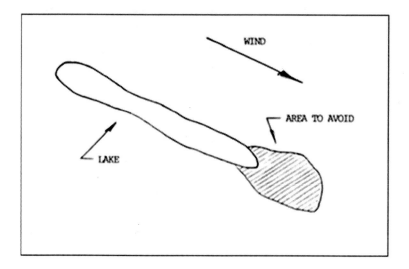

RAIN SHOWERS

On some occasions, a rain shower may save the day. When an overgrown cumulus has reached the stage at which it's producing rain there will often be a row of thermals just ahead of it marked by small wisps of cu. You may also find lift in the rain, actually more often than you might think, but mostly the air will be descending and sometimes at a high rate of speed. As if that isn't bad enough, the performance of most sailplanes degrades significantly when wet.

Most often it pays to avoid rain. If that's not possible, plan on losing a lot of altitude in a short period of time, just to be safe.

Expect dead air just behind a shower. Behind a cumulus nimbus, the entire area will be flooded by cold air, totally void of any convection and may remain so for several hours.

DOWN-WIND SLOPING TERRAIN

Here is a trap you need to watch out for. Don't get caught downwind of down- sloping terrain. The air is displaced from the higher, colder surroundings down to warmer levels, thus stabilizing the air mass, inhibiting convection.

Uphill sloping terrain with the wind on it is fertile ground for thermals, it becomes a desert when the wind blows the other way.

SNOW SHOWERS

From a safety standpoint, beware of snow showers. An innocent light snow shower from an average size cumulus cloud can develop into a monster snow squall with zero visibility in an astoundingly brief period of time. Treat snow showers with a lot of respect.

Once I car towed into light snow flurries, at the top of the launch I lost sight of the field.

> DON'T PART WITH YOUR DREAMS.
> WHEN THEY ARE GONE, YOU MAY STILL EXIST,
> BUT YOU HAVE CEASED TO LIVE.
> **Mark Twain**

OBJECTIVE

HOW FAST

As you leave each thermal, the objective is to get to the *top* of the next as fast as possible. Of the four things you need to know, this is the least important. 'Where to go' and 'When to thermal' have a much greater impact on the average cross- country speed than how fast you fly between thermals.

MACCREADY RING

Back in the early nineteen fifties Paul MacCready derived the optimum speed to fly between thermals, and that speed is based on three things:

1. Performance of the glider.
2. Rate of sink between thermals.
3. Rate of climb in the next thermal.

To establish and display this optimum speed he devised a speed-to-fly ring, consisting of a rotary ring fitted around the variometer face, calibrated for the specific glider's performance. You set the ring to the expected rate of climb of the next thermal and the variometer needle will point to the optimum cruise speed. These circular slide rules have now been replaced by computers, but we still need to enter the rate of climb expected in the next thermal.

AVERAGE RATE OF CLIMB

Don't be misled by the vairometer. The <u>achieved</u> average rate of climb, which is what we are concerned with, is the altitude gained divided by the total time associated with a thermal, including the time spent centering and fumbling, plus whatever procrastinating we do at the top before leaving. Taking all that into account, the net effect is that the actual average rate of climb is about half of the variometer reading during the better part of the climb. Consequently, the correct MacCready setting is half the variometer reading.

MACCREADY SETTINGS AND INTER-THERMAL SPEED

The expected average rate of climb in the next thermal, which becomes the minimum acceptable rate of climb, is referred to as the "MacCready setting". The correct MacCready setting enables the computer to tell you what the optimum cruise speed is between thermals, whether going through sink or lift.

It became customary to select the MacCready setting based on the previous thermal, on the assumption that all thermals are the same on any given day. This works well enough in southwest Texas where all thermals are alike. However, on most days in the eastern part of the country do not expect the next thermal to resemble the one you just left. You will likely do much better by estimating the rate of climb in the next thermal to establish the MacCready setting. Keep in mind, the thermal you just left is history, it is only the strength of the next thermal that matters.

A simpler and very effective method to determine the MacCready setting is to simply set it at the rate of climb you are willing to stop for. If in doubt, it is better to err on the lower side.

When in the thermal from which you anticipate starting the final glide, it does pay to match the MacCready setting with the rate of climb as the computer will then indicate the optimum altitude at which to start the final.

THE PROBLEMS WITH MACCREADY

Attempting to fly at MacCready speeds has its problems. In the first place, unless you have the uncanny ability to predict what the air is doing ahead of you, your timing will be off. On a good eastern day with climbs of 3 kts (that's achieved rate of climb, not variometer reading), following the MacCready speed director as you penetrate the sink surrounding a thermal you will be doing 90 kts by the time you reach it. Entering the thermal, you zoom up to reduce speed. Having reduced the speed in accordance with MacCready, but being a little behind the curve, you will be down to thermalling speed just as you get to the other side of the thermal and before you have decided whether to use it or not. If you elect not to use the thermal, you will be regaining cruising speed while in heavy sink, which will not do much to enhance your performance. Also, the 'G' loads in these zoom-ups conceals the little bumps associated with thermals, making it very difficult to sort things out and figure out what is going on.

Another disadvantage is that attempting to fly at MacCready speeds requires a great deal of concentration which will draw your attention away from the myriad of other things you need to keep track of such as clouds, streeting, wind, terrain, trend in conditions, other traffic, etc., etc. In the eastern part of the country, where the lift varies from thermal to thermal, the MacCready value must be reset constantly.

AN ALTERNATIVE TO MACCREADY

On further investigation it turns out you will do equally well by not varying the speed all that much.

On that same good eastern day, flying a 15 meter glider *(The difference in performance between the different models produced over the past 20 years, 15 Meter or Standard, are not enough to worry about when it comes to cruising speeds.)* you will not go far wrong by maintaining 75 kts, plus or minus 5 kts will not make a whole lot of difference. Favoring the slow side has the advantage of increasing the range, thus giving you a broader selection of thermals to choose from. This, of course, is only advantageous if it leads to the use of stronger thermals. In better weather favor the high side.

The advantage of varying the speed in accordance with the ups and downs are negligible. Even going through heavy sink, 80 kts is about optimum, going much faster will likely reduce your range. An exception to this is when flying in conditions the southwest have become famous for, then the optimum cruise speed may be 90 kts, whether you are in sink or not.

Of course, there are situations where it makes sense to deviate somewhat from these guidelines. If you are heading for a good size, really well defined cu it may pay to speed things up, especially if there already is a glider beneath it climbing like a rocket.

Whenever the vario indicates positive lift slow down to 65 kts, but not any slower until you decide to circle. If you elect not to stop, just ease the stick forward a bit and you will be back to cruising speed. Only when flying along a line of lift will it pay to get down to 60 kts.

There has been much said about dolphin flying, but that requires strong conditions with closely spaced, well defined, reliable clouds – the kind of conditions we are rarely privileged to in the east.

Reference: Soaring Symposia. "The price you pay for MacCready Speeds "Wil Schuemann.

I suspect a good number of our top pilots use the MacCready method, others use it only partially, and some have adopted the 'Alternative to MacCready' method. Yet, they all perform equally well. No doubt, you will eventually settle on a method which works best for you.

BE PREPARED TO CHANGE GEAR

Even it you chose not to adhere to MacCready your mean cruising speed needs to be in accordance with the conditions. In the previous example, the speeds given was for a day with 3 kt thermals. Add a few more knots on stronger days and step it down when thermals are weaker. It is rarely pays to fly below 70 kts.

Conditions may vary throughout any given day, or conditions can be different in some areas along the task. There are days when we fly through two or even three different air masses. It's essential to be on the lookout for changing conditions, and be ready to shift gear. If for instance, the clouds ahead appear to be down cycling, it may be prudent to slow down a little. Several cu in a row with no lift could be an indication of down-cycling. Any sign of over-development is a good reason to be cautious. In extreme cases you may have to hold up and wait for an over-developed area to recycle. Conversely, you may have been in survival mode for a while, but you must be prepared to start pushing again as soon as conditions improve. When crossing a sizable hole of dead air, slowing down to the speed for best L/D is an option to be seriously considered.

> LOVE AND SOARING
> ARE THE CHAMPAGNE OF LIFE.
> AND THUS INTOXICATED, YOUR SOUL CAN
> REACH INFINITE HEIGHTS.

MINIMIZE CIRCLING

WHEN TO THERMAL

The most effective way to improve your average cross-country speed is to minimize circling. Whenever you are circling you are going nowhere. Consequently, you want to be sure that whatever circling you do is worthwhile. Every time we stop for a thermal there will be time spent centering. For this reason it pays to take as few thermals as possible.

DETERMINE MINIMUM RATE OF CLIMB

During the half hour you spend evaluating conditions before heading out, you should decide on the minimum rate of climb you are going to be willing to stop for. Naturally, you must be prepared to change this value in accordance with changing conditions.

ACCEPTABLE RATE OF CLIMB ALSO DEPENDS ON ALTITUDE

Aside from the MacCready setting, your present altitude will also influence your choice of thermals. The closer you are to cloud base, the more selective you should be. Assume that shortly after pushing off at cloudbase after a 5 kt rate of climb you encounter another thermal of the same caliber after only losing 500 ft. You may consider an "S" turn, but anything else would be a waste of time, the most you could hope to gain is a mere 500 ft, while risking losing a few hundred if you turn the wrong way. A Thousand feet further down it may be advantageous to stop for another 5 kt climb but you are too high for a 3 kt thermal, and so forth. Eventually you may get as low as you want to get, in which case you will be willing to stop for anything.

Another situation to guard against is the tendency to hang on to a mediocre thermal from a low save after reaching an altitude at which you would have passed up a thermal of that strength had you encountered it while cruising. Move on until you find a stronger thermal. On the other hand, if you have sampled several thermals, and not found what you are looking for, it may be prudent to take a weaker one to the top.

OPERATING BAND

Theoretically, the operating band is considered to be the upper two thirds of the convection layer. If the maximum altitude is 6,000 ft, the operating band should be between 2,000 ft to 6,000 ft. So much for theory, in real life the general practice is to stay within the upper half. Another factor to consider when establishing your height band is the level of experience. When first starting out, stay on the high side – this tends to be needless advice.

Here are some of the reasons it pays to stay in the upper zone of the convection layer:

- Clouds can better be used when you are reasonably close to them, individual cells are much easier to pinpoint. But don't get too close, visibility is not too good at cloud base, making cloud reading difficult.
- Using clouds becomes impractical when you get low. A cu may look and be active, but the thermal may have expired at the lower level. Furthermore, thermals lean with the wind, and it is not easy to judge the degree of leaning. Incidentally, the leaning is more pronounced closer to the ground, as the column approaches cloud base it becomes nearly vertical.
- Thermals are weaker and not as organized at lower levels. On some days this band below which the climbs are slower and more difficult, can be at an altitude of several thousand feet. Once you discover at what level it is, strive to remain above it.
- When the wind gets up around 25 kts, thermals will be blown apart close to the ground. On such a day it can be very time consuming to get back up.
- A notable shear-line can be troublesome, as well. The thermals may not necessary be all that bad below the shear-line, the problem is that it may be a real challenge to penetrate through it. Once you determine what that level is, it pays to stay above it.
- The depth of convection is another consideration. If the thermals do not go much higher than 2,500 ft, you will probably want to stay in the upper one third.
- As you get lower you cannot be as choosy in thermal selection.
- At 1,200 ft, rule number one is: Don't leave what you have for something better. You may even be losing slightly at first, but nine times out of ten, if you stay with it, the rate of climb will gradually improve, probably due

to the combination of your presence helping to break it free, and your centering efforts. In any case, at that altitude your chances of finding another thermal is slim unless you happened to notice a bird, or sailplane cranked into a tight circle and climbing smartly. If the thermal is drifting into a shady area the thermal is very unlikely to improve. If no other opportunities are in sight, your best bet is to head into a sunny area, or where the sun was a short time ago.

- Unless you have a considerable amount of experience, regard the flight as having ended when you get down to 800 ft, and concentrate on the pattern and landing.

When you do get low keep things in perspective, it's important to think positive. There is no need to get panicky at 2,000 ft. Remember, that's normal release altitude, and how often are you not able to stay up from a 2,000 ft tow? Just pretend you just got off tow. Nor is there need to consider the flight over and done with when you reach 1,200 ft. Think of how many times you have gotten back up from that altitude when flying local.

For 18 years I used only car tows, except at contests. Whenever I got down to a thousand feet or so, I regarded the situation as being at the top of a launch with the world of opportunities before me.

ENTERING A THERMAL, WHEN TO TURN

When you are low, and can no longer afford to be choosy, the best bet is to turn right away. Any hesitation and there is a good chance you may miss the thermal all together. If you turn immediately your circle will at least be in part of the thermal, then commence centering by shifting your circle in small increments so as not to risk losing it.

Remember thermals are smaller near the ground, so you will do much better with well banked turns, about 45°. Steep turns are also safer, as stall recovery can be accomplished quickly and with very little loss of altitude. But to be safe, carry a little extra airspeed. Don't ever perform slow, shallow banked turns close to the ground. That is definitely risky business.

At higher altitudes there are a couple of situations when you should hold off for a few seconds. Naturally you don't want to initiate a turn before reaching your predetermined minimum rate of climb you are willing to stop for. An exceptionally large cu with a broad, alluring, dark base, may give you good reason to believe the lift to be a good deal better than average for the day. In that circumstance, hold off until the rate of climb meets your expectation. When encountering lift that is fairly strong, but not quite good enough to circle in, or you are too high, a figure eight is often a good compromise.

Large clouds are sometimes fed by a single cell and some exploring may be necessary to find it. A word of warning – be careful not to be overly persistent in your search, even though the cloud looks great, whatever you expected to find may have expired. In that case, the sooner you face reality and move on, the better. If you make more than one searching circle it's easy to fall into the trap where your thinking goes something like this: "If I leave now I will have wasted the time I've spent, it must be over here somewhere, I'll just make one more circle, and so on – better to cut your losses and leave.

Some large cu are sustained by several cells. If you suspect there is better to be had than the one you are in, it might be worthwhile to look around. Whenever you find what you are looking for, or it's as good as you can expect it to get don't hesitate, turn immediately and establish an angle of bank of no less than 35°.

If your glider is equipped with flaps, the question is when should you shift them into thermal position? Should you lower them while slowing down as you approach the thermal or wait till you start the turn. There are different opinions on this subject, but I leave the flaps in the cruise position until starting a turn. If I don't stop for the thermal, I leave the flaps alone.

ENTERING A THERMAL ALREADY OCCUPIED

When entering a thermal with other gliders in it, rule number one is, always circle in the same direction. The first glider in a thermal establishes the direction of turn. If you approach a thermal with another glider in it, but he is a thousand feet higher, does it really matter which way you turn? It sure does. The problem is if you circle in the opposite direction, what does the pilot do who later joins up somewhere in the middle? If more gliders arrive there is going to be mass confusion.

Never pull up in the center. This may be the most efficient entry, but dangerous. Be sure to avoid pulling up directly below another glider. It is impossible to predict the gain in altitude due to the combination of slowing from cruising to thermalling speed, and entering the lift. This scenario has resulted in several collisions where a glider entering a thermal pulls up into another glider. When in a thermal, it is extremely unnerving to watch a glider entering below you at high speed, then proceed to pull up from behind and below where you cannot see him. The only thing you can do is brace yourself for the impact.

Keep in mind, as a glider pulls up, the horizontal speed drops off rapidly. Pulling up in front of another glider is a recipe for disaster.

The correct procedure for joining an occupied thermal, whether the other gliders are at your level or not, is to enter tangentially, outside the thermal. Then move in, after having slowed to thermalling speed. The gliders already established in the lift must not be inconvenienced, they should not have to alter their flight path in order to accommodate you.

WHEN TO LEAVE A THERMAL

It is time to push on when the rate of climb drops to two-thirds of the mean. This usually happens a few hundred feet below the top of convection. There are of course times when it makes sense to climb to the top, as when faced with a hole or when approaching deteriorating conditions.

HOW TO LEAVE A THERMAL

The most efficient way to leave a thermal is to tighten the turn when on the opposite side of the circle to the direction you are going, cutting straight through the center on the way out, picking up speed in the process. So as not to compromise safety you cannot use this technique if there is someone else at your level. In any case, cruising speed should be established before entering the sink. Entering the sink that typically surrounds thermals, at minimum speed is expensive in terms of altitude lost.

If you are faced with a sizable hole and you need all the advantage you can get, there is another trick you can use to extract the maximum amount of energy from the thermal. It requires a strong thermal which doesn't weaken at cloudbase. Make a few additional circles at cloud base (500 ft below), converting lift to extra speed before setting course. Remember, no erratic moves if there is someone else with you.

BASE DECISIONS ON WHAT LIES AHEAD

Situational awareness is crucial at all times. Remember, what you do at any given time depends on what the conditions look like on course. As stated previously, always be ahead of the glider. Don't let the glider take you where your brain hasn't been five minutes before.

WHEN LOW

In the interest of safety, when you get down to the 1500 ft. level the most important thing you can do is to turn the radio off. Being low on a cross-country flight will probably provide the most demanding situation you will ever encounter in your flying career. Aside from trying to stay up, you must also go through the process of selecting a suitable field, with the myriad of tasks that entails. You will definitely not be in need of other things to occupy your mind.

The radio will not help you stay up, nor will it help you land. It will only distract your attention from the task at hand at a time when you can least afford it.

On rare occasions I get a chance to fly with my best friend who happens to be a high ranking competition pilot. Whenever he doesn't respond to one of my radio transmissions my heart skips a few beats in joyous anticipation – he always turns off his radio when in trouble.

FEW THINGS ARE HARDER TO PUT UP WITH THAN THE ANNOYANCE OF A GOOD EXAMPLE.

Mark Twain

FINAL GLIDE

First, you need to decide on arrival height. One thousand feet is reasonable. Many pilots use 800 ft, and the brave hearted plan their arrival at 500 ft. When first starting out, plan to get back at whatever height you feel comfortable with. If using a GPS, set the altitude window to read, 'altitude needed to reach destination' rather than 'altitude above sea level,' this makes life a lot simpler.

Preparing for the final glide is one instance where MacCready definitely comes in handy. Set the MacCready value to the rate of climb of the last thermal and the computer will tell you the optimum height at which to leave for home.

In some cases it is prudent to add some additional margin, pending on, how long the final glide is and how the sky looks. On a long final there is a greater chance for things to go wrong than on a short final.

On a long final, say 30 miles, an additional thousand feet makes sense, especially if the day is still active and there are no clouds. Also, keep in mind that if there is a tailwind component your glide ratio will degrade somewhat as you get down in the lower layer where the wind speed decreases. Conversely, if there are clouds, and better yet, streets going in the right direction, it is another matter – no margin is necessary. In fact, many contest pilots when blessed with this situation will start their final glide a thousand feet below glide slope, counting on gaining enough altitude along the way, to make up the difference.

When on a final glide of 10 miles, whatever arrival altitude you have chosen ought to work out just fine. Any further margin would simply prolong the flight.

In short, when deciding on the altitude for the final glide you need to take all the factors into account such as distance, conditions, and wind velocity changes with altitude.

Allow for higher terrain en route, the computer does not take that into account.

Then there is the dreaded 'finger-nail-biting' final glide. In spite of all our planning, things will every so often go wrong, and we find ourselves on final much lower than we want to be. This not only happens during contests when points are at stake, but just as often when flying just for fun. We all know the proper thing to do is to select a field while there is plenty of time and altitude. Nonetheless, if the gauges indicate we should make it back with two hundred feet to spare, it can be very tempting to give it a try.

A fine-tuned final at the end of the day is tricky business. On a marginal final, another couple of hundred would significantly ease your mind, and it is very tempting to try a turn if you hit a little bump. Be careful, more than 50% of the time it doesn't pay off, if there is really nothing there or you turn the wrong way, you can easily lose 200 ft; this is further aggravated if there is a headwind, now you haven't just lost 200 ft, but distance as well. To justify a turn the lift has to be fairly solid, in most cases it pays to simply slow down, or make an 'S' turn through the lift.

When getting closer to home, and the ground, you will be faced with one of the most treacherous situations in gliding. When a few hundred feet above the ground, and the outcome is uncertain it is crucial to have a plan, you need to know exactly where and how to get the glider safely on the ground, at all times. This is an undertaking many good pilots have not handled successfully.

> *DON'T PART WITH YOUR DREAMS.*
> *WHEN THEY ARE GONE, YOU MAY STILL EXIST,*
> *BUT YOU HAVE CEASED TO LIVE.*
> **Mark Twain**

LOW FINISHES

This is one of the most controversial subjects in gliding. There are those for whom crossing the finish line at high speed, followed by a victorious pull-up, is one of the most exhilarating experiences in our sport. Then there are others who consider this maneuver extremely hazardous, and should never be performed.

Perhaps it is because of the controversy that this subject have been shunned in all text books. Regardless, there will be pilots who will not be able to resist temptation, so I believe it's appropriate to cover this subject, and perhaps we can reduce the number of accidents.

- Preparation needs to start several miles out. If carrying water ballast, open the dump valve, you don't want to fiddle with that later.
- Be sure you have plenty of altitude.
- Give the safety belts an extra tuck.
- Be aware of any potential traffic around you.
- Have a firm grip on the stick.
- Beware of getting fixated on the finish line. Thoroughly scan the entire area around the airport. Note any traffic and anticipate where it will be when you get there.
- Plan what your flight path will be after crossing the line. You don't want to arrive at the top of the pull-up wondering what to do next.
- If there are any other finisher behind you, tell them what your intentions are.
- The absolute minimum airspeed to cross the line at is 110 kts.
- If there is any doubt about reaching the minimum prescribed speed, slow down, pull out the spoilers and land straight ahead.
- Be careful not to get too slow at the top of the pull-up. The airspeed drops rapidly when the nose is pointed upwards.

There are three conditions in which never to do a high speed finish:

1. In a brisk tailwind. Pulling up through a wind gradient, going down wind, will deplete the airspeed at an alarming rate, and very little altitude will be gained during the pull-up.
2. High winds and turbulence.
3. Rain. The most common causes of accidents:
4. Lack of planning.
5. Failing to abort a high speed finish and land straight ahead when too slow.
6. Pull-up through a wind gradient, going down wind.
7. Loss of control due to high winds and turbulence.
8. Attempting a full pattern when too low.
9. Spin-in due to inadequate spin training or currency.

I am not aware of any accident having occurred while actually crossing the finish line.

189

EFFECTS OF WIND

KEEP TRACK OF WIND DIRECTION AND STRENGTH

A change in wind direction may influence the relationship of lift to clouds. Also, should you get to the point where you need to evaluate fields you ought to know the direction you will want to land in.

If you need to search for a ridge for a last minute save, knowing if there is enough wind to make the ridges work, and the direction of the wind is obviously essential.

IMPACT ON STRATEGY

Rather than the air moving over the terrain, it may help to think of it in terms of the terrain being on a conveyor belt moving beneath you. Unless you are striving to reach some point on the ground your flying is strictly relative to the air. Whatever speed is optimum for the conditions will be the same whether going downwind or upwind. The only difference is that any inefficiency will be more noticeable when going into the wind.

APPROACHING TURN POINTS

However, there is one situation when the wind direction should influence your strategy and that is when approaching a turn point. The objective is to do as much of the thermalling as possible while drifting on course. Consequently, when approaching a turn point upwind it pays to go into the turn relatively low, but don't overdo it. If going in to a turn point down-wind, get as high as possible just before rounding the turn.

FINAL GLIDE

One situation in which the optimum speed to fly will be influenced by wind direction and strength is when the immediate destination is a point on the ground, as when on final glide. To cover the greatest distance, slow down when going downwind, and additional speed will get you further when going into the wind.

TASK PLANNING

Even on days with light winds there is nearly always some streeting taking place along the wind line. Although streeting may not be discernable and very much disorganized, it can have a positive effect on performance. On legs in line with the wind, attempts to string cu together will require less course deviation, the air between cu will be better, and due to the tilt of thermals it will be easier to connect when approaching clouds upwind or downwind.

When planning a task, align as many legs along the wind line as possible.

RIDGE FLYING

There are excellent publications on this subject, so I will leave that to the experts, except for the following situation which I have not seen covered elsewhere.

When the wind is on the ridge by a mere 10 or 20 degrees it will be deflected by the ridge and flow parallel with it just below the crest, but it may be flowing over the ridge at the very top. If this is the case, sustaining altitude may be possible as long as you stay above the crest, but once you get slightly below the top the game is over.

> SOARING IS FLYING'S MOST NOBLE ART.

HOW TO GET STARTED

TWO-SEATER TRAINING

Making the first cross-country flight in a two-seater with coaching from the rear seat by a qualified instructor is an excellent way to enter the world of cross-country soaring.

On their first cross-country flight most people have three shortcomings that will require some effort to overcome:

1. Not turning steep enough when thermalling.
2. Flying too slow between thermals.
3. Not being selective, stopping for every thermal.

The more local flying you have done, the more ingrained these habits have become, and the more difficulty you will have in overcoming them. It's also possible that your thermalling skills will need some polishing.

WEATHER

Basically, if you can stay up, you can go cross-country. Nevertheless, select a reasonably good day for your first solo, cross-country flight. A day with 3 kt thermals and scattered cumulus at 5,000 ft or so, will do just find. If you are going to wait for the perfect day with 8,000 ft cloud base you will probably never go. Remember, I am talking about the eastern part of the country.

By all means check the weather report. There are several excellent sources on the internet, including Dr. Jack. I just want to point out, in case you haven't already noticed, meteorology is not an exact science. At contests, where we have the best soaring weather forecasters to be found, many glorious days predicted do not come to pass. Conversely, I have seen many days with a totally hopeless forecast, and a dismal looking morning, blossom into a glorious afternoon. If you stay home whenever predictions are not favorable you risk losing out on some fine soaring.

My Diamond distance flights took place on days I should have stayed home, had I believed the forecast.

There are also days when our old standby indicators for a good soaring day do not hold true, such as: The height of cloud base being proportional to the spread between dew point and temperature (predicted high temperature, minus dewpoint, divided by 4.3, multiplied by 1000;) and cool nights followed by high daytime temperatures. Even the most positive indicator of good soaring weather, the passage of a well-defined cold front, can let you down.

It is a good habit to check the forecast, but remember it is only a prediction. The only sure way to find out what the weather has in store is to take a tow. Besides, weak and difficult conditions are wonderful opportunities for some real meaningful practice.

> WEATHER MAN AT A CONTEST: "THIS OVERCAST IS OF NO SIGNIFICANCE TO THIS TASK — IT'S NOT THERE ACCORDING TO OUR CHARTS."

LEAD AND FOLLOW

Following an experienced cross-country pilot around a task is a fabulous learning experience. It does not need to be an official course, but thorough preflight planning is desirable. The procedure to be followed should be clearly understood beforehand. One leader should not take on more than three followers.

OBJECTIVE

- To give you the opportunity to fly a task in the company of an experienced cross-country pilot, gaining practical experience in X-C technique while flying your own sailplane. Learn how to do successful cross-country flying in spite of perhaps less than ideal weather conditions.

ADVANTAGES OVER TWO-SEATER TRAINING

- Although following a leader, some decisions will be yours, e.g. landing out.
- More so than in a two-seater, you will have a sense of responsibility for the success or failure of the flight, which will greatly enhance the sense of

achievement and build confidence.
- Practical demonstration of *your* glider's performance, thus building confidence.
- Demonstrating what *you* can do, with *your* glider will significantly expand your horizons and your enjoyment of the sport.

ON COURSE

- The group must start together, with the leader on the bottom.
- When the group enter a thermal, the leader should spiral down with brakes open to the lowest follower. This procedure should be followed throughout the flight.
- If there is any difference in altitude when it's time to press on, the lead glider should be at the bottom.
- It is very likely the leader will fly through thermals which you normally would not pass up. You must resist the temptation to circle. Even one turn will place you far enough behind to make it impossible to catch up. To get the full benefit of this exercise, it is imperative the followers stay close to the leader. Consider yourself attached to the leader by a long tow rope.
- It is important for the group to stay together, but never fly close behind and just above another glider. Keep in mind, if the glider ahead pulls up in lift, it will also move back relative to your position, resulting in a high risk of collision.
- Flying behind and off to one side of another glider is strategically ideal. It gives you a chance to connect with a thermal he might miss, and if he finds a thermal you can join him. In a contest it is an especially neat place to be if the other pilot doesn't know you are there. But from a safety standpoint it is definitely not advisable. If he finds a thermal and makes a sharp turn toward the side you are on you will immediately be facing one other, head on. Don't ever be in that position unless you are sure he knows you are there, even then it's not recommended.

LOVE AND SOARING
ARE THE CHAMPAGNE OF LIFE.
AND THUS INTOXICATED, YOUR SOUL CAN
REACH INFINITE HEIGHTS.

PRACTICE FOR CROSS-COUNTRY WHILE FLYING LOCAL

First, let's define local flying. Local flying is by no means restricted to the perimeter of the airport. It simply means that we are within glide ratio of the airport with some allowance for the pattern and other eventualities. Even a moderate glide ratio of 30:1 gives us a considerable range to practice in. At 5,000 ft you are still local at 20 miles out; staying upwind provides a further margin of safety.

The objective of practicing is to have as few undeveloped skills to cope with as possible when the time comes for the real thing.

Local flying is generally detrimental to cross-country flying. It is all very well and wonderful to float around at cloudbase over the airport enjoying the view, but you don't learn much. Worse, because there is little incentive to optimize performance bad habits tend to creep in which are not always easy to break.

To be beneficial, each flight should have an objective. Define your weak areas and concentrate on those.

SET ALTIMETER TO SEA LEVEL

Set the altimeter to sea level on all flights. Chances are that when you go cross-country there will be other gliders around. When someone announces being in your proximity at a certain altitude it's nice to be using the same language. Especially on a hazy day.

THERMALLING

If you have done a lot of local flying chances are you probably do not bank steeply enough to optimize your climbs. Of course, there is little motivation to optimize the rate of climb when flying local, after all, as long as you are staying up, there is no incentive to do better. There are no time constraints, you could be in the same thermal all day. Make a genuine effort to get out of that mode and really concentrate on getting the best rate of climb possible out of every thermal. Getting out-climbed from time to time, or failing to stay up when others remain airborne, is an indication there is room for improvement. If you get out-climbed while flying a 1- 26 don't blame it on the glider's performance. Because of its low wing loading a 1- 26 can make very tight circles, enabling it to out-climb everything else. Remember, never be satisfied.

If you favor thermalling in one direction, make it a point to practice your weak side whenever you can. Don't stop working on it till you are equally proficient at turning in both directions. It is a significant handicap to favor one direction of turn over the other. When joining others in a thermal, the direction of circling has already been decided for you. Having a weak side will, at times, discourage you from turning toward the rising wing, as you should when encountering a thermal. At first, most right-handed people favor right hand turns.

> *I WOULD RATHER BE IN MY GLIDER*
> *AND THINK ABOUT GOD,*
> *THAN BE IN CHURCH AND THINK ABOUT MY*
> *GLIDER.*
> **Arne J. Boye-Moeller**

SPEED BETWEEN THERMALS

Almost everyone who have been restricted to local flying maintains the same speed whether thermalling or cruising. Since you are not going anywhere it doesn't seem to make much sense to worry about how fast you are going, even though at times altitude is lost by going too slow when going through areas of sink. On any local flight, make it a point to establish a cruising speed in accordance with thermal strength and sink between thermals.

ALWAYS HAVE A MAP WITH YOU

Orient the map in the direction of flight. Practice map reading, note terrain features and how they relate to the map. Even if you do have a GPS, being able to navigate by map will come in real handy when the GPS stops working someday.

HAVE A CAMERA MOUNTED — IF NO GPS

It should be mounted in accordance with FAI guidelines. Taking turn point pictures is not as easy as you might think. Fortunately, this is something that can be practiced at the home airport and well worth the effort. There are few things more exasperating than making an FAI qualifying flight only to have it rejected due to unacceptable turn point pictures.

Naturally, if your glider is equipped with a GPS there will be no need for this exercise.

LOCATING AND CENTERING THERMALS

To effectively practice locating and centering thermals, limit your climbs to 2,500 ft, then spoiler down to about 1,500 ft and look for another thermal.

Making lazy circles near cloud base is very nice, but it won't do much to improve your soaring skills.

PRACTICE NOT CIRCLING

Take the first thermal to the top. Then see how long you can stay up without circling. This exercise makes you more keenly aware of the conditions and the importance of planning ahead.

This is something you can practice very nicely when flying passengers, in case you are involved with this activity at your club. Passengers generally do not enjoy going around in circles, and if you keep them up for more than 20 minutes or so, they either get sick, bored, or both.

LEAVE THERMALS EFFICIENTLY

Get in a habit of leaving the thermals as soon as the rate of climb drops down to two- thirds. Practice leaving the thermals as you would on a cross-country flight, making a sharp 180° when opposite the point of exit so as fly through the center, picking up speed in the process. Remember, only practice this when you don't have company.

ALWAYS CARRY A BAROGRAPH — IF NO GPS

A barograph trace will show if you exit the thermals in an expedient fashion. The trace at the top of each climb should be in the form of a sharp peak. A trace with rounded tops is a sure sign that you linger too long. It is also important to get accustomed to operating the barograph and preparing the barogram so you no how to do it when it counts.

If you are using a GPS, don't forget to evaluate the vertical trace.

GPS USAGE

If you plan to use a GPS, get well acquainted with it while flying local. Trying to figure out how to operate your GPS on your first cross-country flight is definitely not a good idea.

Furthermore, GPS use on local flights is very helpful. Select your airport as the next waypoint and you will know, at any time, how far you are from the airport, and the height you can expect to arrive at. I know of one incident where a pilot made an unsuccessful field landing 4¼ mile from home. Being over elevated terrain, he got the impression of being too low to make it back. Had he

197

used his GPS (which he never did) he would have known that home was within easy reach.

CONCENTRATE ON EFFICIENT FLYING

Be selective, use only the strongest thermals. It is easy to drift into complacency when flying local. Don't get in the habit of being content with simply staying up.

KEEP TRACK OF CONDITIONS

Keep track of conditions while you are climbing so that you know where to go next before reaching the top of the thermals, just as you would on a cross-country flight.

FINAL GLIDES

Just about everyone underestimate the distance which can be covered from any given altitude. Aside from final glides, knowing the performance of your sailplane is invaluable when crossing blue holes and hostile terrain.

An excellent way to develop this judgment is to make a lot of final glides. Fortunately, final glides can easily be practiced on local flights. In the beginning, start the final glides some 10 miles upwind, and plan to get back with 2,000 ft. As you gain experience and confidence, lower the arrival altitude and start the finals further out. You will be surprised how much practice it takes before you totally believe your sailplane's performance.

MINI TRIANGLES

Practicing triangles with turn points between 6 to 10 miles from the airport is an excellent way to monitor your progress. Establish a start and a finish line and be sure to take turn point pictures, or use a GPS for turn point verification. If you do not validate the turn points, there is a temptation to cheat just a little, and the benefit of the exercise will be lost.

IF YOU WANT TO GROW OLD AS A PILOT, YOU'VE GOT TO KNOW WHEN TO PUSH AND WHEN TO BACK OFF.

Chuck Yeager

FIRST CONTEST

Once you have a number of cross-countries under your belt you ought to consider entering a Regional Contest, but don't enter with the expectation of winning. Your first contest should be regarded as a golden opportunity to gain experience which cannot be gained by any other means. Furthermore, it's simply marvelous to be surrounded by so many people sharing a common interest which also happens to be yours.

When the time comes, do not select a contest where off-airport landings are unduly challenging, you most certainly will land out at one time or another before the contest is over. Previous field landing experience is a must. Your first off-airport landing, and your first contest is not a good mix. One or the other will provide all the stress you could possibly want to cope with. Although your intention is to merely participate, it is easy to get caught up in the spirit of competition and push on when you normally wouldn't, creating a situation for a more challenging field landing.

When it comes to contest strategy, I strongly suggest you read, "The SRA

Guide to Soaring Competition." This is an excellent, 17 page publication published by, and available from the Soaring Racing Association. In addition to that, you should be familiar with the rules.

GOOD REASONS TO ENTER A CONTEST

1. It provides an excellent opportunity to fly cross-country. Tow planes, tow pilots, ground crews, retrieval crews and all the rest of the support needed for cross-country flying are in place.
2. Flying in less than ideal weather, on days you normally would not even consider rigging your glider, you will discover the extent of cross-country flying possibilities in marginal conditions.
3. Flying with other pilots is an excellent learning opportunity.
4. At the pilot's meeting you can learn how other pilots flew the task and what you might have done differently. This constitutes an excellent de-briefing. You will also have gained a much better appreciation for the day's potential.
5. You gain a realistic evaluation of your performance.
6. You will probably learn more during a one week competition than you do in a whole year of flying by yourself.
7. You will have the time of your life.

GRAVITY ISN'T EASY BUT IT'S THE LAW.

About the Author
Kai Gertsen
April 15, 1929 – May 23, 2011

His soaring life began in Denmark, in 1944. Kai was only 15 years old and had little training as he was towed down a grass runway in a SG-38. The primary glider had no instruments, no canopy, no tires, and no dual instruction. You just got in to fly and followed the flag signals from the instructor on the ground. This could have been the extinction of a young boy, but it was only the beginning. For the next 67 years, Kai logged over 6000 hours and 144,700 cross-country miles in a glider. He still holds the NYS Altitude Gain record of 18,047ft, Free Distance record of 350 miles in a Schweizer 1-26, and made two 1000K flights.

Kai's Gliders	Badges
Flat top LK	A,B,C, - Denmark
Ka6-CR	Silver C (#56)
HP-14	Gold C (First one in a 1-26)
Scheumann Libelle	Diamond C (#25 – First in the East)
Discus A	FAI 1000K Diploma - #42
ASW-24	
ASW-20B	
ASW-27	

Acknowledgements

When Kai Gertsen gave me chapter 2, "Discovering Soaring" to read in early January 2011, he joked that "if nothing else, it will put you to sleep." It didn't, and I asked to see more.

This started an intense, three month short collaboration, during which time Kai worked feverishly to finish writing his life story, while courageously fighting his illness. When he could no longer sit behind his computer and write, he dictated on a tape recorder and gave instructions to his daughters Linda and Cindy.

On Kai's behalf, I would like to thank Linda and Cindy for their help in finishing their father's chapter 5 and for searching for files and photographs on his computer. Surely, this was not easy for them. I would like to thank Andy Brayer for proofreading the manuscript and Tim Welles for clarifying some of the more technical parts of the manuscript, when I could no longer ask Kai. Thank you to John Seymour for letting us use his and his father Ed Seymour's pictures, and for his overall support. Garey and Deborah Hudson for their help with the "About the Author" information. And, of course, Helga, for allowing the use of their family pictures, deciphering Kai's handwritten notes, and for her support and strength.

Shortly after I asked Kai to think about a title for this book, he left me a brief message; "I have a title: Desperate to Fly. That pretty much sums up my entire life."

Karin Schlösser
Editor/Publisher